GREAT RELIGIONS OF MODERN MAN

Hinduism

GREAT RELIGIONS OF MODERN MAN

Richard A. Gard, *General Editor*

BUDDHISM

Edited by Richard A. Gard

CHRISTIANITY: CATHOLICISM

Edited by George Brantl

CHRISTIANITY: PROTESTANTISM

Edited by J. Leslie Dunstan

HINDUISM

Edited by Louis Renou

ISLAM

Edited by John Alden Williams

JUDAISM

Edited by Arthur Hertzberg

Hinduism

EDITED BY

Louis Renou

GEORGE BRAZILLER
NEW YORK 1962

For information address the publisher
George Braziller, Inc.
215 Park Avenue South
New York 3

Library of Congress Catalog Card Number: 61-15496

First Printing, October 1961
Second Printing, December 1961

Printed in the United States of America

Acknowledgments

The editor wishes to thank the following for permission to reprint the material included in this volume:

GEORGE ALLEN & UNWIN LTD.—for selections from S. Radhakrishnan, *An Idealist View of Life;*—for selection from S. Radhakrishnan, *The Bhagavad-Gita;*—and HARPER & BROS. for selections from S. Radhakrishnan, *The Principal Upanishads.*

CAMBRIDGE UNIVERSITY PRESS—for selection from R. C. Temple, *The Word of Lalla the Prophetess.*

THE CLARENDON PRESS, OXFORD—for selections from J. Eggeling, *The Satapatha-Brahmana* (Sacred Books of the East);—and for selection from J. Jolly, *The Institutes of Vishnu* (Sacred Books of the East).

E. P. DUTTON & COMPANY, INC.—for selections from the book *Hindu Scriptures,* ed. by Nicol Macnicol. Everyman's Library. Reprinted by permission of E. P. Dutton & Company, Inc.

HARVARD UNIVERSITY PRESS—for selections from W. Norman Brown, trans., *The Saundaryalahari, or Flood of Beauty*, copyright, 1944 by President & Fellows of Harvard College;—and for selections from Franklin Edgerton, trans., *The Bhagavad-Gita,* copyright, 1958 by President & Fellows of Harvard College.

E. L. LAZURUS & COMPANY—for selections from Nicol Macnicol, ed., *Hindu Scriptures.*

LUTTERWORTH PRESS—for selection from W. G. Orr, *A Sixteenth-Century Indian Mystic.*

LUZAC & COMPANY LTD.—for selections from J. Brough, Selections from *Classical Sanskrit Literature.*

THE MACMILLAN COMPANY—for selections from A. L. Basham, *The Wonder That was India;*—and for selection from S. Radhakrishnan, *An Idealist View of Life.*

OXFORD UNIVERSITY PRESS (Bombay)—for selection from E. Thompson, ed., *Rabindranath Tagore;*—and for selections from R. E. Hume, *Thirteen Principal Upanishads.*

ROUTLEDGE & KEGAN PAUL LTD.—for selection from Cowell & Cough, *The Sarva-Darsana Sangraha.*

SIDGWICK & JACKSON LTD. and A. L. BASHAM—for selections from A. L. Bashan, *The Wonder That was India.*

SMITS, N. V. NED. BOEK-EN STEENDRUKKERIJ—for selection from J. A. B. Van Suitenen, *Ramanuja on the Bhgavad-Gita.*

Preface

Passages in this book have been gathered first and foremost from the ancient texts, that is, from among the works on *Śruti* or "Tradition based on Revelation" (Vedic period) and on *Smṛti* or "Tradition based on Memory"; in short, they are generally from Sanskrit literature prior to the twelfth century. Whatever be the interest of certain other texts, either those which are comparatively modern or those written in other languages, Hinduism is precious primarily because of its sources; and these sources are the texts which help us observe the creation or at least the establishment and development of the great spiritual disciplines which are the very foundation of Hinduism. "Edifying" passages from certain works which are classified among belles-lettres have not been excluded, since religious inspiration in India manifests itself through a great variety of spokesmen and interpreters. On the other hand, relatively little material has been taken from works of a technical philosophical nature: to present them exhaustively would have claimed too much space; and after all, what the *darśanas* contain or evoke by way of religious content is to be found already in a more accessible form in the *Upaniṣads,* in the *Purāṇas* and other ancient source books.

In spite of the brevity of quite a number of passages, an attempt has been made to give as complete a picture as possible of the ideas, beliefs and practices of Hinduism. This will be equally evident in those passages extracted from non-Sanskritic works which appear from the seventh century A.D. (religious poems in Tamil) to the contemporary period. It was particularly important that we not set aside those modern movements of thought which reflect what has often been called the "renaissance of Hinduism."

Except in a few isolated cases, extant English translations have been reproduced. First of all, at best only a part of the selections could have been translated by this editor; and it would then have been necessary to retranslate from French into English. Secondly, good English translations are so abundantly available that the only difficulty we might have is to choose among them. And finally, it was not unprofitable to allow the reader to feel, by means of this disparity of styles, the ever-changing aspects of this immense domain where the most divergent literal and literary approaches have their own justifications.[a]

I wish to express here my warm thanks to my former pupil Dr. J. K. Balbir, at present Professor at University College, Naini Tal (India), for having carefully translated into English the Introduction as well as the thirty-seven introductory notices.

L.R.

Paris, March, 1961

[a] By the very fact that various translations have been used, there is a certain diversity in presentation as well as in transliteration of certain customary terms. *Brahmin,* for example, either transliterated as *Brāhmaṇa* or *Brāhman.* It was not considered imperative to maintain an absolute uniformity in this regard.

The lettered footnotes aim at facilitating the study by means of brief explanation of technical terms and proper names.

Contents

A Note on Pronunciation

Among the more unfamiliar letters to be found among the transliterations from the Sanskrit in this volume are the following:

ṛ	pronounced *ri* as in "river"
ś	pronounced *sh* as in "shape"
ṣ	pronounced *sh* as in "shun"
ṅ	pronounced *ng* as in "sing"
c	pronounced *ch* as in "church"

For a more complete pronunciation guide to Sanskrit letters, the reader may consult "Chief Foreign Alphabets," *Webster's New International Dictionary*, Second Edition, p. 75.

Introduction

1. *General Characteristics of Hinduism*

One might at first attempt a geographical definition of Hinduism by recognizing in it the totality of religious forms which originated and developed on Indian soil. It would then be necessary to exclude Buddhism, which in ancient days spread across a large part of Hindustan and still remains very much alive in some areas of the continental borderlands. It would also be necessary to exclude Jainism, which has today about one and a half million followers although in the past it was, relatively at least, more widespread. Other religious groups would also have to be excluded: six million Christians, Jews and Zoroastrians, and some twenty-five million fetishists and animists, who one might say participate in varying degrees in certain elementary forms of Hinduism.

In relation to the mass of the Indian population, which at present numbers approximately four hundred million, these groups are practically negligible both statistically and culturally. This is not the case, however, with Islam. Since the eleventh century Islam has steadily drawn millions of persons from the Hindu community; and even today, in spite of the creation of Pakistan as a Muslim state within the subcontinent, Islam has some thirty-five million followers in the Indian Union. As for Sikhism, or the religion of the Sikhs, it may be considered a religious movement at the extreme limits of Hinduism: it is not considered a heresy.

To confine Hinduism to the circumference of India, however, would be to bypass the missionary character of this religion in the past. In the so-called Hinduization of southeast Asia, Indian religious influences combined with indigenous elements and in the course of time were assimilated by Buddhism, Islam or some form of national religion. In this way Hinduism has had a profound influence, especially in Cambodia, ancient Champa and Bali. One should also recall that there are Hindus in Ceylon (among the Dravidian population), in Nepal, in Pakistan (an inestimable number) and in Indian settlements scattered all over the world.

Can one rather define Hinduism by its elements? Actually, this will have to be done; but in attempting to find such a unifying definition we run the risk of generalizing to such an extent that we fail to grasp the infinite diversity of forms which constitute Hinduism.

The primitive foundation of Hinduism was in part of Indo-European origin; the framework at least was such, while the content was largely indigenous or was modified on the spot. The Aryan tribes which invaded India during the second millennium before our era brought with them a body of religious belief which was already well organized and which survived in classical Hinduism—at the cost of many modifications. This "Aryan" religion (that is, Indo-European on Indian soil) had already been sifted out during the so-called Indo-Iranian intermediary period. It was at the end of this period that a separation occurred between the original religion of Iran (pre-Zoroastrian) and what was to become the Vedic religion in northwestern India.

To this ancient foundation was added a succession of influences which made Hinduism a religion quite different from that of the Aryan invaders. Most of these new developments took place during historical time. The main stages were the appearance of great philosophical speculations and the fixation of the *Smṛti* (at the beginning of the Christian era), the first fragmentation into sects (first and second centuries A.D.), the appearance of *bhakti* (*ca.* 600-800 A.D.), and Tântrism (since 800 A.D.). The main outline of all these movements existed, however, as early as the Vedic period.

It is possible, too, and even probable that Hinduism assimilated some pre-Aryan, or at least non-Aryan institutions which were inherited from local cults and modified with the primitive Indian data as the basis. The prehistorical civilization of the Indus basin (Mohenjo-Daro and Harappa), which dates from the beginning of the second millennium before Christ, testifies to some of the characteristics by which we can identify a proto-Hinduism: an image of the Mother Goddess, a horned god in the posture of a Yogin, and ritual emblems of vegetal or animal character.

Hinduism is indeed a complex and rich religion. No founder's initiative, no dogma, no reform have imposed restrictions on its domain; on the contrary, the contributions of the centuries have been superimposed without ever wearing out the previous layers of development.

In fact, according to what phenomena one considers, Hinduism can appear either as an extrovert religion of spectacle, abundant mythology and congregational practices or as a religion which is profoundly interiorized. To the first view belong the activities of the sects, the *bhakti* movement, and the worship of the cow, in which some find the concrete symbol of Hinduism; here, too, could be included the principle of nonviolence, at least in its social application. To the view of Hinduism as an interior life belong the paths of spiritual progress, the quest for liberation, the tendency to renunciation, and finally the intensive concentration on problems which in other cultures are more often reserved for theologians or philosophers. Hinduism, which is eminently popular in its practices and external manifestations, is essentially also a religion of the learned: it cannot be understood if the *Vedānta* and the *Sāṃkhya* have not been fully comprehended or if, at the outset, there is no idea of the immense network of symbolism which underlies and links together all Indian thought.

Finally, Hinduism characterizes society as a whole. The caste system with its various "stages" of existence is part of Hinduism. Life is looked upon as a rite; there is no absolute dividing line between the sacred and the profane. In fact, there is no Hindu term corresponding to what we call "religion." There are "approaches" to the spiritual life; and there is *dharma,* or "maintenance" (in the right path), which is at once norm or law, virtue and meritorious action, the order of things transformed into moral obligation—a principle which governs all manifestations of Indian life.

When, it may be asked, did Hinduism begin? A reply to this question can only be indirect: Hinduism began at the time when the original activity of the Vedic ritual came to an end, when the old Vedic framework was lost. We may date this occurrence, perhaps, between the sixth and fourth centuries B.C. From this perspective, a text or a religious manifestation is designated as Hindu as long as it does not reveal any trace of division into schools or of the ancient liturgical patterns. Such was the position immediately before our era of the Epics, the ethico-juridical literature and the Aphorisms (*Sūtras*) which served as the basis for grand speculations.

The situation, however, is not quite so clear, for just as there was an undercurrent of Hinduism in Vedism, so there are Vedic survivals in classical Hinduism. The name of "Brāhmanism" is sometimes given to the oldest of the learned forms of Hinduism. But taking everything into consideration, it is preferable to look upon Hinduism as a whole without looking for superficial subdivisions. On this interpretation Vedism is considered the most ancient form of Hinduism. Certainly Vedism cannot be neglected since all that follows it is inexplicable without it.

If we are to look for a global characterization of Hinduism, we could (as was recently suggested) consider it the very type of a religion of renunciation. Certainly Hinduism could exist without those who renounce, but it would remain singularly impoverished and would be as if deprived of its crest. Many of the elements of the religion seem to have been created for the man who has withdrawn from mundane life, or they were later modified for his needs. This could explain the evolution of the theory of *karman* and of transmigration, perhaps too the development of *bhakti* and (by a kind of reversal) of Tântrism. On a general plane, we can consider as effects of renunciation both Indian pessimism and the escapist tendency, which may go so far as to reject the elementary exigencies of religion. It is all an affair of the individual. Hinduism does not know the opposition which is found in Buddhism between a well-developed monastic milieu and a secular environment; consequently, a Hindu, even if he belongs to a group, considers himself alone to be responsible for his salvation.

2. *Vedism*

It has been said that Hinduism turned its back on Vedic beliefs. If this is true, it is just as reasonable to claim that Hinduism is a continuation of the Veda. Not only did the Veda offer in an embryonic state the majority of the characteristics which developed with the passage of time, but also classical Indian mythology would scarcely be assimilable without the Veda, in which private rites as well as much Hindu speculation have their source.

The Vedic religion consisted first of all of a very highly developed mythology. Its pantheon lacked an absolute sovereign and distributed gods according to the regions occupied by them, according to their relation with rites, and according to the functions which they represented (ethico-religious gods, war gods, gods of the "economy"). The general tendency was to attribute highest importance to the god who was being invoked by conferring on him those attributes which commonly belonged to other gods. Still, there were gods who permanently occupied an honored and lasting place. First among these was Indra (and his associates, notably the twin gods *Aśvins*). Indra was a doer of warlike deeds who drove back darkness, killed the demon, and protected the Āryas, being the "Ārya" god par excellence. Then, among the major gods, there were two complementary deities personifying sacrifice: Agni, god of fire with its divers forms, and Soma, god of plant and liquor.

Man addressed prayers to the gods, asked of them material goods and a long life. He knew, however, that in and above the gods there were abstract forces which were active. Notable among these was *Ṛta*, the force of order which correlated the cosmic and the human. The profound meaning of Vedic prayer was precisely to maintain order: to watch carefully the normal course of natural phenomena so that by imitating these natural patterns, the ritual cursus might guarantee perenniality.

This mythology and its underlying speculations are known through the *Ṛg-veda,* a difficult text which contains hymns addressed to the gods. This text, which may be dated from the middle of the second millennium B.C., is the most ancient literary document of India and one of the most ancient of the Indo-European world. It is composed in very archaic Sanskrit.

Texts later than the *Ṛg-veda* reveal other aspects of the religion. Magic, or more correctly prayers of a compelling purpose, is the subject of poems contained in the *Atharva-veda,* a text which is probably a little later than the *Ṛg-veda* in origin. This text also contains the most ancient traces of cosmogonic speculation. Yet even in the comparatively recent portion of the *Ṛg-veda* is to be found the theme of the primitive man, a sort of cosmic giant who was immolated at the time of the First Sacrifice. Out of his limbs originated the human and animal species, notions and things. This is the archetype of Indian myths of creation.

Other collections contain formulas to be recited during the course of ceremonies. And along with these formulas (which are often borrowed from the verses of the *Ṛg-veda*), there are explanations and commentaries to clarify their usage. These commentaries are the main subject of the texts called *Brāhmaṇas*, of which the most important is the *Brāhmaṇa of the Hundred Paths* (*Śatapatha Brāhmaṇa*).

There are, in addition, formulas and commentaries adapted to more secret practices, those which take place in the silence of the forest. It is in these that we find the beginning of that esoteric teaching which later was to play such an important part in India. In these, too, is found the path toward the world of those dedicated to Renunciation.

Most of the texts, however, beginning with the *Ṛg-veda*, were composed with a view toward sacrifice. Sacrifice was at the center of the Vedic religion: a succession of oblations and prayers, fixed according to strict liturgy, in which the culmination was reached when the offering was placed in the fire. The objective of the ritual was to enter into communication with the divine world and thence to acquire certain advantages which profane initiative could not enjoy. Sometimes vegetable, sometimes animal, the offering consisted predominantly of the Soma plant, from which is extracted a liquor which possesses intoxicating qualities.

There were no prayers disassociated from cult; there were neither temples nor idols; but there existed a body of paid priests who during the performance of the ceremony put themselves at the disposal of the patron and his wife while they participated in the ceremonial. The scenario varied greatly from a simple daily oblation in the fire (*Agnihotra*) to the sacrificial sittings in which the king celebrated his victories in majestic manner

(*Aśvamedha:* horse sacrifice) or was anointed at the time of his coronation (*Rājasūya*). Private rites were performed by the head of the family with a restricted liturgy at the family hearth.

Description of all these practices is preserved in the *Sūtras*, which are texts of aphoristic style (solemn or private, strictly religious or semijuridical). These texts, like the whole of Vedic literature, are the property of special schools, each of which has its own practices and refers to different portions of the ancient canon.

We can form only an imperfect idea of such a religion whose past extends over centuries without any clear evidence of an evolution. Certain aspects of the religion, especially its socio-cultural context, remain obscure. Although it does not disregard interior ritual or asceticism, it is primarily a ritualistic religion in which the believer defines faith as the conviction he has of the exactitude and effectiveness of the rite. Moral obligation demands the exercise of good acts, of giving ("Give in order to receive"). Many of the primitive values of restraint and of the exchange of goods have been preserved in the Vedic religion. On ultimate ends and future life there is no clear perspective: during the period of the *Brāhmaṇas* men beg that they may not "die again."

Toward the end of what is generally called the Vedic period, that is, toward the fifth or fourth century B.C., there appeared new texts, the *Upaniṣads* or "Equivalences." Without abandoning ancient modes of thought, these texts reveal a sort of gnosticism which attempts to explain by way of parables that the *ātman* or individual soul is identical with *brahman* or the universal soul.

"Thou art That": that is to say, "Thou, the individual, art identical with the ultimate principle of things." This is the supreme truth which leads to Liberation. Thenceforth the world of the gods, the external apparatus of cult, which had already been strongly reduced in the *Brāhmaṇas*, tended to disintegrate. We discover an allegorical ritualism, a religious form of an introspective type. This form endured in the background of later religious manifestations in India and nourished an entire current of Hinduism. In its origins it was a sort of avant-garde among the circles of the professional ritualists.

After the *Upaniṣads*, a popular Hinduism flourished. Suddenly we encounter a religion open to all tendencies, one which in many respects was more akin to primitive Vedism with its luxuriant mythology than to the semi-esoteric Vedism of the *Āraṇyakas* and the *Upaniṣads*.

3. *Texts of Hinduism*

Ever since the last centuries before our era, texts containing religious thought followed one upon the other. For a long time they were written in only one language, Sanskrit, but it was a Sanskrit which was progressively modified and simplified in comparison with the oldest Vedic language. During the first millennium of our era, Tamil—a language of the Dravidian family—was used, and, secondarily, Prakrit. During the second millennium other Dravidian languages and the neo-Indian dialects originating from Sanskrit appeared. Finally, during the last century and a half, the English language was added to all these. In comparison with the extraordinary diversity of languages utilized for the expression of Buddhism, Hinduism has had a relatively moderate linguistic expansion.

The texts form the primary basis of our knowledge of the history of Hinduism. As a secondary source, there are from time to time the records of foreign travelers. These firsthand observations of religious practices and their appeal to the intimate sentiments of the believers serve to renew our knowledge of religious facts.

For the ancient periods we have to take into consideration archaeological data, inscribed or engraved pillars, mural paintings, underground or open-air sanctuaries, or temple-cities. Iconography, which was abundant from the seventh or eighth century A.D., supplements what literature has to teach us regarding details of mythical stories and the symbolism of divine acts and attributes. In southeast Asia, notably at Angkor, Hindu statuary may be found which at times reveals new religious motifs.

While certain *Upaniṣads* show a discrete beginning for Hinduism, the massive eruption of the religion was formed by the Great Epics, above all by the *Mahābhārata*, a text which, at least in its contents, is certainly prior to our era. It is a sort of unbalanced Iliad: warlike narratives are mingled with mythological scenes and moral discourses. In its text are treated all of the deepest values of Hinduism on the ethical and the juridical plane, the duties of the individual in himself and in his relation to society. Its culmination point is the *Celestial Song* (*Bhagavad-gītā*), which has been called the Evangile of Kṛṣṇaism. It is a kind of sermon addressed to the hero Arjuna by Kṛṣṇa, his comrade in arms: Kṛṣṇa reveals himself as no other than the Supreme Being, guardian and guarantor of all human actions, the originator of those methods which lead to spiritual insight.

The Epics find their natural continuation in the *Purāṇas* or "Antiquities," which are huge compilations dealing with religious practices, mythology and cosmogony. Mingled with these strictly religious elements are a number of more secular subjects. The *Purāṇas* are a major source of semipopular Hinduism. In contrast to the Epics, the *Purāṇas* have been diversified according to the sects, or at least according to a certain mythico-ritual order which served to frame the later sects. In more recent times, their counterparts are the *Saṃhitās*, which are Vaishnavite in character; the *Āgamas*, which are rather Shaivite; and the *Tantras*, which, when they do not maintain their generic meaning of "Sacred or Ritualistic Books," signify more specifically those texts relating to the so-called Tântric aspects of Hinduism.

A result of the comprehensive character of Indian religious phenomena is that certain texts which we would classify among belles-lettres or didactic literature constitute from a certain point of view a direct testimony of Hinduism. Among the didactic works a separate place should be reserved for philosophy. What are rather incorrectly called philosophical systems have been considered by the Indians as different paths to the mystic life or different approaches to Liberation even when they commence with rational postulates of logic, deterministic evolutionism or rational interpretation of the sacred texts. From the point of view which interests us here, the most important of these *Darśanas* or "visions" are the *Vedānta,* which attempts an explanation of the coexistence of the Absolute and the phenomenal world, and the *Yoga,* which describes the way to mystic control. Such basic texts have led to the creation of a vast literature which is characterized by the predominance of "commentaries." Some of these commentaries, as those relating to the *Gītā* and to the "Vedic" *Upaniṣads,* have been compiled during the contemporary period.

The Tamil language came on the scene especially with the Nayanārs and their Shaivite hymns of the seventh century and with the Āḷvārs who composed at about the same time a "Tamil Veda," which was oriented toward Viṣṇuism. In Tamil, as in other languages of the south, adaptations of Sanskrit works have been numerous. A new accent is found, however, with Vêmana in the fifteenth century, who advocates in his poems a religion devoid of external practices. Among the literatures which developed from Sanskrit, one finds imitations of the old sources and sometimes too there are signs of a new spirit. Gradually an independent literature developed which was popular in style and consisted chiefly of hymns as well as a collection of sermons. The greatest names here are from the linguistic domain of Hindī: Kabīr, who in the fifteenth century introduced a rather personal mystical vision; and Tulsīdās (16th–17th centuries), who freely utilized the ancient Sanskrit Epic and became the apostle of devotion to Rāma.

The renaissance of Hinduism during the nineteenth century brought about a tremendous increase in the number of didactic works written in English. During the same period there was a continuation of the traditional practice of composing prayers, gnomic or fable literature in Hindī, Bengāli, Marāthī and eventually in Sanskrit once again.

4. *Practices and Beliefs*

Ritual in the strict sense of the term lost its importance after the Vedic period; the old ceremonies fell into disuse, their modern reflections being purely archeological demonstrations. On the other hand, external practices increased in importance. There was also a notable breaking down of the relation between myth and ritual, which during the ancient period had been closely associated. A wide diversity of procedures of worship reflects the diversity of approach toward the Divine.

Unknown in ancient periods, the cult of the idol gained momentum with the development of monumental iconography. To fashion the idol of a god, to install it in the sanctuary, to treat it as "animated," to anoint it: all of these became major rites. Worship, or *pūjā*, is the central point of religious activity. The rite consists of welcoming the god as a distinguished guest. Bathing the god, dressing him, adorning him and applying scent, feeding him, putting flowers round him and worshiping him with moving flames accompanied by music and song: such are some of the essential features of the rite. The idol is taken out of the temple in a procession which furnishes the occasion for scenes which mingle mythology with themes of folklore. Taking place in the temple, this type of ceremony is public; it carries no obligation for the individual. For some, perhaps for the majority, the idol is the god himself, and we can classify this as idolatry; for others, symbolical values are true values and the idol is nothing more than what it is in any form of cult in which the sacred is incarnate in some concrete form.

Descended from the household hearth of olden days, the temple may range from the modest village sanctuary with its crude idols to the religious cities which encompass within their walls a whole cycle of activities and the mountain temples which aim to reproduce the cosmic mountain Meru, pivot of the world. The temple is dedicated to a particular god. The image of this god is accompanied by a particular attribute which can become autonomous. In the Shaivite context, for example, this attribute is often a *liṅga*, a phallic emblem, which is perhaps of distant non-Aryan origin. The *liṅga* is a short pillar of black stone, bare or engraved, around which is performed *pūjā* of a votive character.

The existence of the temple presupposes a permanent clergy whose position in the social hierarchy ordinarily remains quite inferior. Here and there in history can be found evidence of a system of *devadāsīs* (sacred courtesans and danseuses) attached to the temple. There exist also a body of domestic priests who are permanently or temporarily attached to a family either as spiritual teachers (*guru*), as secular teachers (*ācārya*) or as astrologers.

Quite different from these is the *Saṃnyāsin*, or the "renouncing individual," who holds himself aloof from social life and does not participate in religious practices. He has either chosen the path of detachment since youth or has given himself to the "dispassionate" path (as prescribed by ancient texts) after having passed through the other stages of life. He is called *Sādhu* if he is independent; *Svāmin*, if he belongs to some order; *Yogin*, if he practices Yoga.

The idol is not necessary for the representation of a god. We have already mentioned the existence of *liṅga*. There are, in addition, many other, nonfigurative emblems such as the more or less complex geometrical patterns (*yantra* or *maṇḍala*) which are used primarily in Tântrism.

The worshiper, at least in the elaborate forms of cult, submits himself to considerable preparation: preliminary ablutions, food restrictions which may extend to the fast, corporal postures and gestures of the fingers (*mudrā*), control of the breath, "possession" (*nyāsa*) by the god of the body of the worshiper, etc. The notions of the pure and the impure are everywhere evident: purity is perhaps the essential watchword of Hinduism and its religious practices of purification are infinitely diversified.

Prayer consists of the silent recitation (*japa*) of sacred formulae (*mantra*) which are repeated indefinitely. The *mantra* are composed of from one to a hundred or more syllables. Here we find a tribute to the word as form, for many of the syllables (notably in the religious practices of Tântrism) have no meaning while others consist of a simple mention of the divine name such as "*Rām*(*a*)! *Rām*(*a*)!" This type of prayer is an aid to mental concentration and is thought to bring about the desired effects of protection, fulfillment of promise or expiatory virtue.

Other elements of personal worship are the study of the Scriptures, and above all, meditation. Strengthened by Yoga exercises, meditation can lead to such a paroxysm of tension that the exercitant can accomplish the ultimate aim proposed in all Indian religious thought: a state of union with the Absolute.

Those religious practices performed at home are the only ones which are relatively obligatory. Prayer three times a day (at morning, noon and evening) is accompanied by offerings to the gods, to sages and to ancestors. In actual practice these religious activities are appreciably shortened. According to the periods, more elaborate ceremonies are held in memory of ancestors (of three direct generations on the male and female side) with offerings of water and sesame; the object of this is to transform an indifferent or even pernicious dead soul into one who is useful and helpful.

The "sacraments" (*saṃskāra*) constitute another series of personal rites. It is chiefly in these that we find the surviving elements from the Vedic period. In modern times the customary sacraments concern birth, initiation into the Brahmanic life, marriage and death. Inasmuch as a young boy belongs among the "twice-born," initiation marks his entry into Hindu society. This ceremony, like most others, consists of the worship of fire in a manner similar to that of the *pūjā*.

Agricultural, collective and commemorative rites are numerous. Still more numerous are the "vows" (*vrata*) which are restrictions or types of activities to which an individual submits himself freely at a fixed time in order to attain a certain religious merit or to obtain a definite object which he desires.

Among the collective celebrations which are held either in the temple or in its surroundings mention may be made of the feasts or festivals (*utsava*): for example, the worship of the goddess Durgā which lasts for nine days in October; the Festival of Lights (*Dīvālī*) which occurs about the same time; *Holi,* the Spring Festival in honor of Kṛṣṇa. From time immemorial crowds of pilgrims from one end of India to the other have assembled at certain privileged places (one can actually draw a map of sites and routes with their relative importance). The Ganges is considered the most sacred place, for it contains in itself the virtue of numerous *tīrthas* or "fords" which crystallize the manifestations which are sought. On the Ganges it is Benares above all which attracts the attention of the devotees. But here as elsewhere imagination can come into play: any stream of water may be called Ganges, be it only as much as is contained in a jug, and this is sufficient under certain conditions to obtain the same benefit as can be had from a long pilgrimage. Pilgrimages themselves may be occasioned by personal motives, by concern for fulfillment of a vow, or they may arise with one of the anniversaries of great commemorations interspersed throughout the Indian calendar.

It is scarcely necessary to recall that Hinduism includes certain elements typical of a popular cult: worship of trees, of serpents and of special "genii" (which are often of demoniacal nature as in the case of the goddess of smallpox). Magic, too, is widely practiced as are astrology and other forms of mantics.

Thus far we have chiefly been describing the Hindu cult of Vedic origin which includes religious practices of a relatively simple and open kind. Different from this, at once more democratic and yet more closed, is the

Tântric cult: more democratic because it is in principle open to all men and women whatever their social class; more closed, however, because it entails an initiation—or rather, various degrees of initiation classified according to the qualifications of the postulant. It is here, above all, that the help of a *guru* or spiritual master is necessary. Worship of the idol is performed according to a complex procedure; substitutes and symbols are extremely elaborate. In its extreme form, the so-called "leftist Tântrism" or "Tântrism of the left hand," which is evidently reserved for only a minority of followers, we observe the inversion of the normal worship and common ethical principles in favor of certain objects and unusual practices: wine, flesh and free sexual intercourse. The fact that these objects are "worshiped" is evidence that the stage has been passed at which they would be considered sinful. Tântrism is, under certain forms, the antithesis of religion; it is also an exceptional leaven to stimulate mysticism. The practice of Yoga is intensified and is subdivided into Yoga of Formulas, Yoga of Postures, Yoga of "Absorption" and "Royal Yoga"—the last two forms being reserved for those who have transcended the path of action and who hope to obtain an immediate realization of self.

Religious belief is rooted in the divine milieu, the attributes and symbols of the gods. Hinduism is fundamentally polytheistic, not only at the exoteric level but also in the speculative order where the role of the concrete and the figurative god is never abolished. Doubtlessly there are variations in this feeling for a plurality of gods. The philosophers combine it (on another plane) with a belief in one supreme principle, sometimes personified as Lord (Īśvara), sometimes conceived as a neuter deity or an impersonal Absolute (Brahman). This absolute principle may itself be composed of a "qualified form" (*saguṇa*) which is at times considered to be of prime importance while at others is reduced to the level of "inferior knowledge." The common believer is not conversant with the notion of divine unity, which belongs rather to the sphere of the philosophers and is not represented in any direct cult. For the nonphilosophers, diversity appears normal. From this diversity the believer selects his chosen god (*iṣṭadevatā*); his choice implies that he recognizes the importance of other divine forms such as the divine couples or *parêdres*. Such a choice is concomitant with the hierarchization which can be observed in the *dharma* on the social, moral or ritualistic planes.

The number of gods is considerable. India could, in fact, be considered saturated with the divine, a land with an undeniable tendency toward pantheism or, as has been suggested, toward pan-en-theism. Nevertheless, major distinctions have become necessary and are recognized. A sort of trinity, for example, is recognized in Brahmā, Viṣṇu and Śiva. Brahmā (masculine correlative of the neuter *brahman*) is the principle of creation in the universe, Viṣṇu that of preservation and Śiva that of destruction. From the viewpoint of worship, however, this distinction does not have precise significance. Brahmā is a god who does not have great following; rarely has a temple been dedicated to him or a sect been formed in his name. Viṣṇu and Śiva, on the other hand, are deities of the first order. Vedic in certain of their fundamental characteristics, Viṣṇu and Śiva have developed by successive modification until they have been sufficiently deprived of their personalized aspects so that, not without reason, they have at times been called "social principles." With Viṣṇu, the solar god of old, has been combined the form of Vāsudeva, a type of hero, and of Nārāyaṇa, a cosmic god resting on the serpent Śeṣa. Later arises another aspect of Viṣṇu: he appears as Kṛṣṇa, chief of a clan and hero of innumerable exploits. The worship of Kṛṣṇa seems to have given stimulus to the *bhakti* movement. With Viṣṇu are associated the *avatāras*, the incarnations of the god on earth at different periods under the guise of an animal or a human being. These periodic descents of the god to earth are intended to save our world from some great peril. The essence of Hindu mythology has been preserved in the narrations of these *avatāras*, the number of which has classically been fixed at ten: fish, crocodile, boar, man-lion, dwarf, Rāma-with-an-axe, Rāma (the epic hero of tremendous religious implication), Kṛṣṇa, the Buddha, and finally Kalkin or "the incarnation to come." The worship of Viṣṇu reveals the agreeable and happy aspects of Hinduism. In fact, as a religion in the strict sense of the term, Hinduism can almost be summarized as Viṣṇuism.

Different from Viṣṇu and far more complex is the form of Śiva. In him are concentrated the majority of those elements which emphasize the frightful and the fearful aspects of belief: the struggle against the demons and against Evil, the image of Death, the most severe types of asceticism, Tântrism, intellectual knowledge and its dangerous effects. One of the most venerated forms is that of the Dancing Śiva: his is a cosmic dance which proclaims the end of the world. Or there is the ascetic Śiva in the position of a Yogin.

Goddesses who in the past played only a secondary role are now endowed with singular significance. Even the notion of Energy (*śakti*) is superimposed on the time-honored figures of the Mother Goddess who, as Śiva himself, reveals both a gracious aspect (as in Umā) and more often a terrible aspect (Durgā, Kālī). The majority of these feminine concepts are combined with the cycle of Śiva, but at the same time they have been endlessly popularized: there is scarcely anything in common between the supreme Śakti, the wife of Śiva, who in Tântrism reduces her husband to a corpse, and the goddesses of the villages who endlessly multiply and diversify the female principle.

Among the male gods who belong to the Shaivite cycle, at least one is very much in popular favor while still lending himself to esoteric interpretations: he is Gaṇeśa, "master of the troupe of Śiva." He it is who removes great obstacles. His brother Skanda is primarily worshiped in southern India under the name of Subrahmaṇya; this is one of the few points in which one might speak of a "Dravidian" mythology distinct from the common mythology.

If the nature worship of the Veda retreated on all sides, there remained in ancient Hinduism a cult of the planets (including the moon) and especially a cult of the sun. The latter was inherited from Vedic times and later, at the beginning of our era, was rejuvenated as a consequence of Iranian influences. In addition, certain Vedic gods persist, receive new labels and are subject to new mythical episodes. An example of this may be found in the division of space among eight Lokapālas, the guardians of the world who correspond to eight directions.

Royal dynasties are supposed to be descended from heroes of time immemorial; moreover, the royal functions were at different periods subject to deification as represented by combinations of the images of the Sun, of Indra and of the cosmos. Finally, the cult of illustrious personages whether of legend or history and the cult of the saints became attached to the structures of the various sects.

As far as demigods go, those genii of the heavens, the waters, the earth, the atmospheric and the subterranean world, their activity caused little interference for the gods, slightly more for humans. At no stage of development were the demoniacal forms clearly individualized. They all form part of the simple principle of evil which is rather a double-edged principle never established as absolute evil. Literature describes hell and its graded spheres of terrifying tortures. Is there eternal condemnation? True hell is rather a return to earth. More indefinite still are the traits assigned to paradise. On the other hand, the theory of the four ages of the world, the representations of the earth and the cosmos, have been developed with fantastic imagery, giving a background of infinite time and immense space to notions which in the Veda enjoyed but a limited horizon.

What exactly is the import of these gods? "Ethnographical" explanations may have their value, showing, for example, an evolutionary development from the prehistoric prototypes common to many religions. But what must be considered of far greater importance is the specific Indian character, the very sentiments of the Indians. And this is expressed as much in the ancient texts as in the consciousness of those among the living who, looking far beyond all appearances, agree to communicate their intuition. Such explanations are symbolic in nature (how could they be otherwise?) and at first they run the risk of appearing arbitrary. The problem is to retain those traits which reflect a certain consistency; these enable us to discover the appeal of the great divinities, which is certainly complex but coherent. But the variety of attributes and the outburst of monstrous forms require elaborate explanations which are finally more or less contingent.

According to well-known opinion, the divine world is a part of *māyā*, that force of illusion which leads us to believe in our phenomenal world. Truth is to be found beyond the phenomenal; but *māyā* is also conceived of as a positive force, at least by those who admit a pluralism of qualities if not of substances.

Philosophy in India involves men; it aims at practical results. Thus it constitutes an approach toward religion or, better still, is an integral part of religion. The philosophical credo of Hinduism is contained in the *Darśanas,* which are traditionally six in number, grouped in twos. Those systems which developed outside of the six *Darśanas* (and there have been such) all have a more or less clear connection with one or the other of the *Darśanas.* All of the systems offer as an ultimate object the search for the means to attain Liberation, which is conceived sometimes as absence of rebirth and at others as fusion with the Absolute.

The *Sāṃkhya* is fundamentally atheistic and recognizes only Spirit and Nature as the eternal principle of things from which are derived by evolution the totality of forms and beings. Liberation is "isolation"; the soul is de-individualized. The Yoga, which is theistic, retains from the causal cycle of the *Sāṃkhya* only those psychic structures by means of which it teaches psychophysiological control, a restraining of the circulation of thought. This restraint by Yoga makes possible not only the acquisition of superhuman powers but also and essentially the attainment of mystical control. The technique has astonishing mechanical forms which betray perhaps its shamanistic origins; but it is perfectly appropriate for its purpose and is the most highly developed method imaginable for opening the way to intense forms of contemplation. Studied through the *Sāṃkhya-Yoga*, Hinduism appears as a discipline of the unconscious.

In dealing with Indian thought, however, it is the *Vedānta* which is of primary concern. Vedântic thought is based on the old lines of the *Upaniṣads* concerning the relations of the self and the Universal Soul. According to *Śaṅkara* (8th–9th centuries), the founder or restorer of radical nondualism, the only reality is *brahman*, nonqualified essence composed of being and consciousness. *Ātman*, or individual soul, is identified with *brahman*. There is, however, an empirical level of thought which suggests a *brahman* qualified in plural forms: this is the sphere of nescience and illusion. Properly religious accretions, like meditation on the texts and worship, are simple adjuncts. Liberation consists rather in recognizing the identity between *ātman* and *brahman,* or better still, in "realizing" this identity in the self. This Liberation is possible, in principle, after death; but there exists a class of privileged living beings who achieve the unique status of the "absolved life."

Other Vedântic schools mitigate the extreme position of Śaṅkara, admitting (at least with Madhva) a sort of fundamental dualism. The most notable of these schools are that of Rāmānuja and the school of "distinctive non-dualism," in which *brahman* is invested with remarkable qualities and serves as a basis for worship. Rāmānuja opens up for philosophy the riches of the religious quality of worship; philosophically, or at least theologically, it justifies *bhakti,* the affective participation of man with a personal god. Undoubtedly, the origins of *bhakti* go back to a very remote period, but its emotive resources were fully exploited only by thinkers and poets of the Middle Ages. Some of them created the idea of an "abandon" to the Divine, a concept similar to that of grace in Christian belief. They distinguish between the "method of the cat" and the "method of the monkey": in the first method, God saves man without man's participation just as the cat takes its kittens by the skin of the neck; and in the second, a personal effort is needed as when a little monkey clings to its mother to escape some difficulty. According to Rāmānuja, Liberation is achieved variously by good acts, by knowledge and by sensible evocation of the Divine.

Hinduism, then, may be characterized as a system of the means appropriate for the attainment of Liberation.

There is a great variety of such means. At times they are considered mutually related as degrees in a hierarchy of means; in no case, however, can they exclude each other. The way of action is at times regarded as the lowest path: a Vedic heritage, it consists in such acts as external practices, acts of giving and attentiveness to teaching. Disinterested action, however, is exalted to the level of the most valuable efforts. Higher than this is placed the practice of austerity, the "consuming by heat" (*tapas*) which is so frequently described in the literature. This austerity is the essence of Indian asceticism. There is also the Tântric path based, as we have seen above, on a kind of release of inhibitions, even on a reversal of values. The path of knowledge results from an integrated reflection and is transformed into spiritual realization. There are finally the paths of Yoga and of participating devotion (*bhakti*).

The nonliberated man is subject to common destiny: enslaved by his actions which follow him indefinitely, "as the calf follows its mother," he is condemned to be reborn; and as most human actions are tainted by malice, the risk of being reborn in a lower condition, ultimately as an animal, is greater than the possibility of achieving an exalted state. *Karman* (action, or rather consequence of action) and *saṃsāra* (cycle, or indefinite transmigration of living beings) are the elements in Hinduism at the esoteric level which most resemble religious dogmas; that is, they are postulates based on a conviction which is not open to discussion. Existence (life) flows as a torrent; man suffers passively the necessity of death in order that he be born and die, again and again. This is the basis of Indian pessimism, this frightful retributive accountability. But there is an essential corollary: by his actions man can, to a certain extent, direct his destiny. Actions which determine later stages can create fruits which ripen in exact proportion to what the original action was like. Thus ethics receives its place in a religion in which human initiative at first appeared to be miserably impotent: man is urged to perform meritorious acts. Evidently, however, it would be still better to cease to act at all, to exhaust all the reserves of *karman*. Hence the prime importance of renunciation, the inherent negativism of Indian experience. But as life and religion need to be reconciled, forms of activity such as active devotion have been recommended which are not crude in their nature. It is here that Hinduism regains that simple human quality which has proved effective and even capable of creating new values, when in our times as of old it responds vigorously to the exigencies of its political and social vocation.

5. *Religious Sects*

However much one may be tempted to reduce Hinduism to a unity, it is impossible to pass over the phenomenon of the religious sects. In some ways the sect is the reality of Hinduism and shapes its history. The remainder is generalization.

It is not necessarily a question of exclusive groups, much less in general of hostile groups. First of all, there are the very comprehensive denominations, those by which Hindus are divided into Vaishnavites (*Vaiṣṇavas*) and Shaivites (*Śaivas*); *Śāktas,* the third large branch, can be treated as a subdivision of the Shaivites. Sects commence within this global classification. Even the *Smārtas* (the followers of *Smṛti* or "Unrevealed Tradition"), who are supposedly free of sectarian tendencies, have adopted discriminating features. The temptation to form a group is great in India. The scale of sects is the religious counterpart of the system of castes, with this remarkable difference that while theoretically castes include the entire society, sects have never constituted more than islands of relatively slight numerical significance within Hinduism as a whole.

A sect adheres to a specific part of tradition: it recognizes a special basic text as its own; it adopts a particular speculative system; but it neither isolates itself from the totality of the system nor rejects the common postulates. Such, at least, is the general situation. We might consider as sectarian those people who elaborate and refine select values borrowed from the treasury of beliefs; or those who reject a part of recognized usages; or those who manifest exclusivity in their recruitment and a certain element of defiance. At one extreme are the Mahānubhāvas of Mahārāṣṭra who do not accept the Veda and preserve very few of the positive data of Hinduism. The prototypes of these semiheresies (it is quite difficult in India to be completely heretical) are Buddhism and Jainism. These are movements which have always remained separate from Hinduism, although in time they have been impregnated by many influences from Hindu forces surrounding them. Since the appearance of these very old sects, such schisms have never taken place again.

In a certain sense sects are clerical organizations. They often tend to distinguish between the laity and the religious, a distinction generally unknown to common Hinduism. We have exact information regarding religious orders in only a small number of cases. In the ninth century, for instance, we find a case of ten fraternities which were supposed to have been founded by Śaṅkara; their supreme head was called "Preceptor of the World." Monastic communities are frequently mentioned in the literature. We are well informed about their structure in southern India, especially from the thirteenth century on. In modern times the Order of Ramakrishna, founded in 1899, was inspired by Western monastic rule.

The deciding factor for the creation of a sect is naturally the initiative of a master who preaches and explains the scriptures. The type of these founders is repeated throughout history as if by historical law. Under the influence of enlightenment, a man breaks with his past, starts preaching a new doctrine, and after many ordeals succeeds in gathering around himself a body of disciples from among whom shall be found his successor. After his disappearance, his biography is shrouded with legends: here lies the great influence of a *guru* on the Indian mind.

Many of these movements tend to become reform movements. In contrast with popular Hinduism, which became a little stagnant and stale, the sect has become an instrument of progress. Reforms are of different kinds: sometimes strictness in the performance of religious practices is recommended; sometimes protest is registered against social scales and prohibitions in order that every man may have easy access to the religious life. The India of the sects differs, therefore, in its aspirations toward uniformity of belief from the India of the *Śāstras* ("Normative Treatises") which advocates social divisiveness. It is perhaps because of this tendency toward unanimity, which was destined later to be established in the sects, that ever since the proto-historical period the Dravidians subscribed to Hinduism and joined the Brahmanical system; and that, at a later date, a Brahmanical corps was formed in Cambodia. On the linguistic level, the sects have helped in the propagation of the vernacular, while learned India remained anchored to the Sanskritic tradition.

It is difficult to say when the sects came into being. One is tempted to trace their origins to that period of intense fermentation and theological controversy which in the fourth or fifth century B.C. marked the beginning of Buddhism and Jainism as well as the development of the *Upaniṣads*. One might imagine perhaps that the Buddhism of the *Hīnayāna* (Small Vehicle) furnished the impetus for this fragmentation of Hinduism: but this remains hypothetical. We must rather come down to the beginnings of the Christian era, when we find a Greek ambassador, Heliodorus, referring to *Bhāgavatas* as a class of devotees who worship the "Lordly" form of Viṣṇu. Some episodes in the Epics mention a few names of the sects, notably those of *Pāśupatas*. But the fact is that we know few precise details about the history of the sects before the end of the ninth century. At the beginning and until the eleventh century the domination of Shaivism was noteworthy; then Viṣṇuism came to the fore and seems to have preserved its supremacy until modern times except in those territories still loyal to a certain Shaivite primitivism and in Bengal where *Śāktas* have preserved a powerful stronghold. It is Shaivism as well which set foot in southeast Asia around the seventh century and gave place later to Viṣṇuism (at least in Cambodia): a replica of the ebb and flow in continental India.

Thanks to what we know about sects we can attempt to trace in broad outlines the evolution of Hinduism. The descriptions by the Greek Megasthenes in the fourth century B.C. testify to a state of confusion. Actually, we are prevented from observing the true extent of Hinduism at that period by the patronage accorded to Buddhism by the Mauryas and much later by many Indo-Greek sovereigns and by many Kuṣāṇas who were inclined to constitute a state religion. Hinduism was given official patronage only in the fourth century A.D. with the Guptas, the first of the great indigenous dynasties. This resulted in what has been called the "renaissance of Hinduism," which was characterized also by the restoration of Vedic ceremonies. But this notion of "renaissance" is exaggerated, for there is nothing to indicate that in the prior period Hinduism had been deeply encroached upon by Buddhism or that it had undergone any internal degeneration. It is, however, with the first centuries of our era that the great speculative orientation of Hinduism developed.

Toward the end of the Guptas period could be placed the constitution of the *Śākta* doctrines (with the *Śākti* cult) and the beginnings of Tântrism. Philosophical controversy sprang forth in the eighth century, a period which marks the final decline of Buddhism in India and the diffusion of *bhakti*. It was perhaps on Dravidian soil that *bhakti* received its decisive impetus and was nourished by the religious enthusiasm of the *Āḷvārs* and the Nayanārs. In the north of India, Viṣṇuism became the privileged vehicle by virtue of its sentimental effusions (sometimes colored by eroticism), to which the "edifying" stories woven around Kṛṣṇa lent themselves.

The Muslim conquest, which was progressive and partial, did not modify the general aspect of Hinduism; at most, we note the appearance of some mixed movements such as Sūfism. To the credit of Islam should be assigned, indirectly, the acceleration in the growth of sectarian groups, whose maximum vitality can be found between the thirteenth and the middle of the sixteenth centuries. The salient events are the teachings of Kabīr and the syncretism represented by them, and the appearance of what have been called "the reformed sects," such as the military theocracy of the Sikhs (15th–16th centuries), which borrowed many elements from doctrines which are fundamentally Hindu, like those of Kabīr and, beyond Kabīr, of Rāmānanda. In the seventeenth century Tulsīdās presided over the consolidation of the live forces of devotion in the whole of northern India; his name evoked the establishment of new sectarian groups based on the name of Rāma.

In more recent times, sects appeared to be gradually declining and Hinduism tended to assume its old form. In this way perhaps the ground was well prepared for the "revival" of Hinduism, as it is generally recognized, with the beginning of the nineteenth century. This revival coincided with the study in Europe of the sacred texts of Ancient India and, above all, with the gradual growth of Indian national sentiment. A necessarily Indian phenomenon, Hinduism could not fail to display both the virtues and the excesses of any nationalism.

A series of enterprising men, some of them extremely gifted, became apostles of a Hinduism which had been rethought, purified and liberated of its fantasies while at the same time they consolidated its connection with a humanistic interpretation of the *Vedānta.* Among these modern personalities the only common element is their dynamism; their differences are remarkable. Many demonstrate the conscious or unconscious influence of Christianity (Rāmmohun Roy, Keshab Chandra Sen) or more generally of Western culture (Tagore). Some of them insist on a return to the Veda (Dayānanda), but it is a Veda flexible to the needs of our times; others restrict themselves to mysticism (Rāmakrishna), to explanation

(Aurobindo) or to theosophical propagation (Vivekānanda); many are inclined toward social (Rānade) or political (Tilak, Gāndhī) problems. The old formula of *āśramas*, or "hermitages," has been revived, ranging from the phalanstery to a semimonastic brotherhood.

Hinduism can be conceived as faithful to its scriptures (for almost everyone the *Bhagavad-gītā* remains the Book par excellence), while at the same time it is the very type of universalizing belief. All religions are true, we are told, but Hinduism condenses them all by preserving such of their characteristics as may be acceptable to all. Thus there is no more question of mythology or ritual: an outline of general ethics is drawn up, and though not permitting any real concessions as regards the essential, an attempt is made to approach "similar souls" beyond the frontiers of India. The Hinduism which is "exported," one might say, paradoxically elevates a predominantly ethnic faith to the rank of a panhumanistic religion.

The Indian mass is hardly touched by these movements, at least on the religious plane, although social and, above all, political events have left a profound mark on it. It is because of this fact that there has been a cleavage and that concepts free from aggressive overtones have been able to flourish in India.

6. *Indian Society*

Omnipresent and mingled with ethico-social ideals, Indian religion signifies first of all *dharma* as a totality: this is the "eternal" *dharma* of the philosophers. From the demographical perspective, however, *dharma* is fragmented according to castes and "stages" of life: there is a *dharma* for each individual insofar as he forms part of a certain group. This is the special characteristic of the Indian principle of "the one in the many." The same principle is operative in the relation between the sect and Hinduism as a whole and in the fact that penal law has as its counterpart many "vows" and religious expiations.

As regards the "stages" (*āśrama*), or modes of life, the rules laid down for the Student are different from those prescribed for the Householder; and these have little in common with those guiding the life of the Anchorite (third stage) and still less with the rules concerning the Renouncing Individual (fourth stage). This scheme is normative, but it is based on experience. Many Indians, even in modern times, have broken all connections with the world to live their lives in renunciation; others, without abandoning their social obligations, have it is said, "transcended the *āśramas*" and achieved the status of the "absolved life."

More important still is the gradation of society into four classes. At the top of this hierarchy are found the three āryan or free classes, which are theoretically dominated by the Brahmins, who exercise spiritual power; then come the Kṣatriyas, who wield secular power; finally there are the Vaiśyas or artisans, cultivators, etc., who represent the economic aspect (according to the old tri-functional scheme). These three classes comprise the "twice-born" who obtain a second birth through initiation. Apart from these three groups are the Śūdras, somewhat like serfs who nevertheless maintain certain rights. Below these and, one might say, apart from society is the mass of the "impure" or untouchables, of whom ancient literature has little to say but whose existence at all epochs is undeniable even if its membership has varied. These classes are diversified by their privileges, which negatively interpreted form as many prohibitions. On the religious level, the existence of classes signifies that the formal relation of each individual with the Divine is established by birth. Actually, participation in worship differs for the Brahmin and the other twice-born, is reduced to little for the Śūdra, and is completely absent among the outcastes.

By "crossing" among the four classes, eventually even between a member of these classes and an untouchable, are created mixed unions which involve a degradation. The normative texts teach that in this lies the origin of the multiplicity of castes—approximately three thousand in modern times—which divide the Hindu population into fragments. The castes are characterized by many prohibitions concerning partaking of meals outside the group (or admitting members of other groups to partake of one's meal) and marriage outside the group; they are also characterized by more specifically religious recommendations concerning purity and very elaborate practices of purification. If the caste theory is observed, there are few details of existence which are not affected by membership in a caste and few traits of caste which are not definitely of a religious significance. Beyond the restrictions outlined above, there are also relationships determined by spiritual bonds which do not admit of external marriage.

Another classification of men, one which is purely theoretical, is that based on the three phases of human activity: *dharma* or moral activity (the highest), *artha* or interested activity, and *kāma* or playful activity. These three ends reflect, in part at least, the three functions. They are subordinate to a fourth end: *mokṣa* or Liberation.

7. *Conclusion*

If Hinduism is studied superficially or unilaterally, one might be tempted to see in it a chaos of irrational religious practices and superstitions and a degradation through magic and verbalism. The economic dysfunctions engendered by certain religious prohibitions or by the entire caste system have been pointed out. The caste system has been held responsible for social stagnation, while extensive criticism has been offered of negative tendencies, excessive nonviolence and certain deplorable customs such as the burning of widows in past time and child marriage, which is still sometimes practiced. It is evident that there is both good and evil in a religious context which has been allowed to go its own way for more than two thousand years without any internal checks while it retained an attitude approaching defiance which became even more audacious in the face of the temptations offered by the modern world.

But ambivalence is characteristic of India: for her, what is the good of killing her cows if she has to lose her soul? A factor in social and psychical equilibrium is found in the notion of *dharma* with its rigorous justice and the "truth" which it implies (the Indians insist on the attitude of truthfulness as others insist on an "attitude of consciousness"). An important consequence of this is tolerance, nonviolence considered an active virtue; this is a manner of acting which must be respected—even in the political sphere—*regardless of the attitude of others.* In this perhaps is to be found the most spectacular contribution which India has made to the modern world and the most worthy reply to Marxism and its materialism.

Doubtless, Hinduism lacks something of that spirit of charity which abounds in Buddhism, for example. In his concern for purity the Hindu tends rather to keep aloof than to give himself. At least Hinduism has that greatness which is to be found in its search for the equilibrium and harmony which are so characteristic of its institutions. Far from being an intellectual game, philosophy is for Hinduism a spiritual experience: it invites one less to thinking than to cultivating a presence. The relationship between the philosopher and the world is that of a sort of fascination.

The individual is de-emphasized not only because he is an anonymous member of a group which itself forms an integral part of another group, but above all because the great religious objectives are conceived for a situation other than that of an individual in society. These religious objectives touch the individual who has escaped from social life precisely by abolishing his very individuality. Thus, religious facts tend to be translated into a world of symbols, those "secondary" forms which are often more interesting than our direct transcriptions of reality.

Hinduism, however—except perhaps in certain Tântric systems—is not esoteric. By the very fact that there is possibility of choice among diverse paths and various techniques, Truth is for Hinduism an indivisible treasure; spiritual immediacy is widely distributed, the mystic path is open to everyone. In its purest forms, this religion becomes a type of wisdom, that wisdom which impressed the ancient Greeks when they visited India and which could be of some fruitfulness again for our blasé cultures. It is as wisdom that we should like to define Hinduism rather than by the equivocal term *spirituality*.

One is never bound to predict the future; and today the future of a nation is no longer in its hands alone. Still it is likely that the Indian caste system will disappear sooner or later and with it will disappear certain crude Indian institutions. There will survive then a way of thought freed of social contingencies, one which will be endowed with unforeseen powers of maturity.

Selected Texts

A. Sanskrit Sources

I. The *Ṛg-veda*

This text presents a collection or an anthology of about a thousand hymns addressed to principal gods of the Vedic pantheon. The hymns are attributed to individual "authors," but that is unwarranted. The language is a very archaic Sanskrit, and the compilation of the poems should be placed between 1500 and 1200 B.C.

Along with the homage rendered to gods, and mythological or ritual descriptions, we find formulas utilized by poets to invite a god to participate as a distinguished guest in the sacred offering. Some of the compositions are of an entirely different character, notably the many speculative poems: No. 6, for example, the famous poem on the creation of the world; or No. 4, which describes the Primordial Sacrifice, consisting of the immolation of the gigantic man (Puruṣa) from whose limbs have come forth all beings.

1. *To Viṣṇu*

I will declare the mighty deeds of Viṣṇu, of him who measured
out the earthly regions,
Who propped the highest place of congregation, thrice setting
down his footstep, widely striding.

For this his mighty deed is Viṣṇu lauded, like some wild beast,
dread, prowling, mountain roaming;
He within whose three wide-extended paces all living creatures
have their habitation.

Let the hymn lift itself as strength to Viṣṇu, the Bull, far-striding, dwelling on the mountains,
Him who alone with triple step hath measured this common dwelling-place, long, far extended,

Him whose three places that are filled with sweetness, imperishable, joy as it may list them,
Who verily alone upholds the threefold, the earth, the heaven, and all living creatures.

May I attain to that his well-loved mansion where men devoted to the gods are happy.
For there springs, close akin to the wide-strider, the well of meath in Viṣṇu's highest footstep.

Fain would we go unto your dwelling-places where there are many horned and nimble oxen,
For mightily, there, shineth down upon us the widely-striding Bull's sublimest mansion.[1]

(1.154)

2. *To the Waters*

Forth from the middle of the flood the Waters—their chief the sea—flow cleansing, never sleeping.
Indra, the bull, the thunderer, dug their channels; here let those Waters, goddesses, protect me.

Waters which come from heaven, or those that wander dug from the earth, or flowing free by nature,
Bright, purifying, speeding to the ocean; here let those Waters, goddesses, protect me.

Those amid whom goes Varuṇa the sovran, he who discriminates men's truth and falsehood—
Distilling meath, the bright, the purifying; here let those Waters, goddesses, protect me.

[1] For numbered Translation References, see pp. 245 ff.

They from whom Varuṇa the king, and Soma, and all the deities drink strength and vigour,
They into whom Vaiśvānara Agni entered; here let those Waters, goddesses, protect me.[1]

(7.49)

3. *To Dawn*

She hath shone brightly like a youthful woman, stirring to motion every living creature.
Agni hath come to feed on mortals' fuel. She hath made light and chased away the darkness.

Turned to this all, far-spreading, she hath risen and shone in brightness with white robes about her.
She hath beamed forth lovely with golden colours, mother of kine, guide of the days she bringeth.

Bearing the gods' own eye, auspicious lady, leading her courser white and fair to look on,
Distinguished by her beams, Dawn shines apparent, come forth to all the world with wondrous treasure.

Dawn nigh will wealth and dawn away the foeman: prepare for us wide pasture free from danger.
Drive away those who hate us, bring us riches: pour bounty, opulent lady, on the singer.

Send thy most excellent beams to shine and light us, giving us lengthened days, O Dawn, O goddess,
Granting us food, thou who hast all things precious, and bounty rich in chariots, kine, and horses.

O Dawn, nobly-born, daughter of heaven, whom the Vasiṣṭhas[a] with their hymns make mighty,
Bestow thou on us vast and glorious riches. Preserve us evermore, ye gods, with blessings.[1]

[a] Name of a family of poets.

4. *The Puruṣa Sūkta* (*Hymn of Man*)

A thousand heads hath Puruṣa, a thousand eyes, a thousand feet.
On every side pervading earth he fills a space ten fingers wide.

This Puruṣa is all that yet hath been and all that is to be,
The lord of immortality which waxes greater still by food.

So mighty is his greatness; yea, greater than this is Puruṣa.
All creatures are one-fourth of him, three-fourths eternal life in heaven.

With three-fourths Puruṣa went up; one-fourth of him again was here.
Thence he strode out to every side over what eats not and what eats.

From him Virāj[a] was born; again Puruṣa from Virāj was born.
As soon as he was born he spread eastward and westward o'er the earth.

When gods prepared the Sacrifice with Puruṣa as their offering,
Its oil was spring; the holy gift was autumn; summer was the wood.

They balmed as victim on the grass Puruṣa born in earliest time.
With him the deities and all Sādhyas and Ṛṣis[b] sacrificed.

From that great general Sacrifice the dripping fat was gathered up.
He formed the creatures of the air, and animals both wild and tame.

From that great general Sacrifice Ṛcs[c] and Sāma-hymns[d] were born;
Therefrom were spells and charms produced; the Yajus[e] had their birth from it.

From it were horses born, from it all cattle with two rows of teeth:
From it were gathered kine, from it the goats and sheep were born.

When they divided Puruṣa, how many portions did they make?
What do they call his mouth, his arms? What do they call his thighs and feet?

The Brâhman[f] was his mouth, of both his arms was the Rājanya made.
His thighs became the Vaiśya, from his feet the Śūdra was produced.

The moon was gendered from his mind, and from his eye the sun had birth;
Indra and Agni from his mouth were born, and Vāyu from his breath.

Forth from his navel came mid-air; the sky was fashioned from his head;
Earth from his feet, and from his ear the regions. Thus they formed the worlds.

Seven fencing-sticks had he, thrice seven layers of fuel were prepared,
When the gods, offering sacrifice, bound, as their victim, Puruṣa.

Gods, sacrificing, sacrificed the victim: these were the earliest holy ordinance.
The mighty ones attained the height of heaven, there where the Sādhyas, gods of old, are dwelling.[1]

(10.90)

[a] Female counterpart of the male principle, Puruṣa.
[b] Saints and prophets of old.
[c] Stanzas of the Ṛg-veda.
[d] Stanzas of the Sāma-veda.
[e] Ritual formulas of the Yajur-veda.
[f] The four social classes.

5. *To Prajāpati*

In the beginning rose Hiraṇyagarbha,[a] born only lord of all created beings.
He fixed and holdeth up this earth and heaven. What god shall we adore with our oblation?

Giver of vital breath, of power and vigour, he whose commandments all the gods acknowledge:
The lord of death, whose shade is life immortal. What god shall we adore with our oblation?

Who by his grandeur hath become sole ruler of all moving world that breathes and slumbers:
He who is lord of men and lord of cattle. What god shall we adore with our oblation?

His, through his might, are these snow-covered mountains, and men call sea and Rasā[b] his possession:
His arms are these, his are these heavenly regions. What god shall we adore with our oblation?

By him the heavens are strong and earth is stedfast, by him light's realm and sky-vault are supported:
By him the regions in mid-air were measured. What god shall we adore with our oblation?

To him, supported by his help, two armies embattled look with trembling in their spirit,
When over them the risen sun is shining. What god shall we adore with our oblation?

What time the mighty waters came, containing the universal germ, producing Agni,
Thence sprang the gods' one spirit into being. What god shall we adore with our oblation?

He in his might surveyed the floods containing productive force and generating worship.
He is the god of gods, and none beside him. What god shall we adore with our oblation?

Ne'er may he harm us who is earth's begetter, nor he whose laws are sure, the heavens' creator,
He who brought forth the great and lucid waters. What god shall we adore with our oblation?

Prajāpati! thou only comprehendest all these created things, and none beside thee.
Grant us our hearts' desire when we invoke thee: may we have store of riches in possession.[1]

(10.121)

[a] Golden germ, a name for god Brahmā.
[b] Name of a mythical river.

6. *The Song of Creation*

Then was not non-existent nor existent: there was no realm of air, no sky beyond it.
What covered in, and where? and what gave shelter? Was water there, unfathomed depth of water?

Death was not then, nor was there aught immortal: no sign was there, the day's and night's divider.
That one thing, breathless, breathed by its own nature: apart from it was nothing whatsoever.

Darkness there was: at first concealed in darkness, this All was indiscriminated chaos.
All that existed then was void and formless: by the great power of warmth was born that unit.

Thereafter rose desire in the beginning, Desire, the primal seed and germ of spirit.
Sages who searched with their heart's thought discovered the existent's kinship in the non-existent.

Transversely was their severing line extended: what was above it then, and what below it?
There were begetters, there were mighty forces, free action here and energy up yonder.

Who verily knows and who can here declare it, whence it was born and whence came this creation?
The gods are later than this world's production. Who knows, then, whence it first came into being?

He, the first origin of this creation, whether he formed it all or did not form it,
Whose eye controls this world in highest heaven, he verily knows it, or perhaps he knows not.[1]

(10.129)

7. *To Brahmaṇaspati*[a]

He, lighting up the flame, shall conquer enemies: strong shall he be who offers prayer and brings his gift.
He with his seed spreads forth beyond another's seed, whomever Brahmaṇaspati[a] takes for his friend.

With heroes he shall overcome his hero foes, and spread his wealth by kine: wise by himself is he.
His children and his children's children grow in strength, whomever Brahmaṇaspati takes for his friend.

He, mighty like a raving river's billowy flood, as a bull conquers oxen, overcomes with strength.
Like Agni's blazing rush he may not be restrained, whomever Brahmaṇaspati takes for his friend.

For him the floods of heaven flow never failing down: first with the heroes he goes forth to war for kine.
He slays in unabated vigour with great might, whomever Brahmaṇaspati takes for his friend.

All roaring rivers pour their waters down for him, and many a flawless shelter hath been granted him.
Blest with the happiness of gods he prospers well, whomever Brahmaṇaspati takes for his friend.[1]

(2.25)

[a] Or Bṛhaspati, the deity in whom the action of the worshiper upon the gods is personified.

8. *To Varuṇa*

Sing forth a hymn sublime and solemn, grateful to glorious Varuṇa, imperial ruler,
Who hath struck out, like one who slays the victim, earth as a skin to spread in front of the sun.

In the tree-tops the air he hath extended, put milk in kine and vigorous speed in horses,
Set intellect in hearts, fire in the waters, the sun in heaven and Soma on the mountain.

Varuṇa lets the big cask, opening downward, flow through the heaven and earth and air's mid-region.
Therewith the universe's sovran waters earth as the shower of rain bedews the barley.

When Varuṇa is fain for milk, he moistens the sky, the land, and earth to her foundation.
Then straight the mountains clothe them in the rain-cloud: the heroes, putting forth their vigour, loose them.

I will declare this mighty deed of magic, of glorious Varuṇa, the lord immortal,
Who, standing in the firmament, hath meted the earth out with the sun as with a measure.

None, verily, hath ever let or hindered this the most wise god's mighty deed of magic,
Whereby with all their flood, the lucid rivers fill not one sea wherein they pour their waters.

If we have sinned against the man who loves us, have ever wronged a brother, friend, or comrade,
The neighbour ever with us, or a stranger, O Varuṇa, remove from us the trespass.

If we, as gamesters cheat at play, have cheated, done wrong unwittingly or sinned of purpose,
Cast all these sins away like loosened fetters, and, Varuṇa, let us be thine own beloved.[1]

(5.85)

9. *The Liberality*

The gods have not ordained hunger to be our death: even to the well-fed man comes death in varied shape.
The riches of the liberal never waste away, while he who will not give finds none to comfort him.

The man with food in store who, when the needy comes in miserable case begging for bread to eat,
Hardens his heart against him—even when of old he did him service—finds not one to comfort him.

Bounteous is he who gives unto the beggar who comes to him in want of food and feeble.
Success attends him in the shout of battle. He makes a friend of him in future troubles.

No friend is he who to his friend and comrade who comes imploring food, will offer nothing.
Let him depart—no home is that to rest in—and rather seek a stranger to support him.

Let the rich satisfy the poor implorer, and bend his eye upon a longer pathway.
Riches come now to one, now to another, and like the wheels of cars are ever rolling.

The foolish man wins food with fruitless labour: that food—I speak the truth—shall be his ruin.
He feeds no trusty friend, no man to love him. All guilt is he who eats with no partaker.

The ploughshare ploughing makes the food that feeds us, and with its feet cuts through the path it follows.
Better the speaking than the silent brahman:[a] the liberal friend outvalues him who gives not.

He with one foot hath far outrun the biped, and the two-footed catches the three-footed.
Four-footed creatures come when bipeds call them, and stand and look where five are met together.

The hands are both alike: their labour differs. The yield of sister milch-kine is unequal.
Twins even differ in their strength and vigour: two, even kinsmen, differ in their bounty.[1]

(10.117)

[a] Name of a priest, supervisor of the sacrifice.

10. *To Night*

With all her eyes the goddess Night looks forth approaching many a spot:
She hath put all her glories on.

Immortal, she hath filled the waste, the goddess hath filled height and depth:
She conquers darkness with her light.

The goddess as she comes hath set the Dawn her sister in her place:
And then the darkness vanishes.

So favour us this night, O thou whose pathways we have visited
As birds their nest upon the tree.

The villagers have sought their homes, and all that walks and all that flies,
Even the falcons fain for prey.

Keep off the she-wolf and the wolf; O Night, keep the thief away:
Easy be thou for us to pass.

Clearly hath she come nigh to me who decks the dark with richest hues:
O morning, cancel it like debts.

These have I brought to thee like kine. O Night, thou child of heaven, accept
This laud as for a conqueror.[1]

(10.127)

II. The *Atharva-veda*

The *Atharva-veda* is slightly less ancient than the *Ṛg-veda:* but in nature, it is quite different. It is a collection of versified prayers or hymns, some of a magical or an allegorical character, others dealing with cosmogony. The latter compositions develop speculative material which appeared in some of the "recent" hymns of the *Ṛg-veda.* Among the former figure two texts which we present here: one, a prayer to Varuṇa as god of Cosmos (a prayer which ends with a magical imprecation); the other, a charm against fever.

1. *To Varuṇa*

The great guardian among these gods sees as if from anear. He that thinketh he is moving stealthily—all this the gods know.

If a man stands, walks, or sneaks about, if he goes slinking away, if he goes into his hiding-place; if two persons sit together and scheme, king Varuṇa is there as a third, and knows it.

Both this earth here belongs to king Varuṇa, and also yonder broad sky whose boundaries are far away. Moreover these two oceans are the loins of Varuṇa; yea, he is hidden in this small drop of water.

He that should flee beyond the heaven far away would not be free from king Varuṇa. His spies come hither from heaven, with a thousand eyes do they watch over the earth.

King Varuṇa sees through all that is between heaven and earth, and all that is beyond. He has counted the winkings of men's eyes. As a winning gamester puts down his dice, thus does he establish these laws.[2]

(4.16)

2. *Against Fever*

May Agni drive the Fever away from here, may Soma, the Press-stone, and Varuṇa, of tried skill; may the altar, the straw upon the altar, and the brightly-flaming fagots drive him away! Away to naught shall go the hateful powers!

Thou that makest all men sallow, inflaming them like a searing fire, even now, O Fever, thou shalt become void of strength: do thou now go away down, aye, into the depths!

The fever that is spotted, covered with spots, like reddish sediment, him thou, O plant of unremitting potency, drive away down below!

Having made obeisance to the Fever, I cast him down below: let him, the champion of Sakambhara,[a] return again to the Mahāvr̥ṣas![b]

His home is with the Mūjavants, his home with the Mahāvr̥ṣas. From the moment of thy birth thou art indigenous with the Balhikas.

When thou, being cold, and then again deliriously hot, accompanied by cough, didst cause the sufferer to shake, then, O Fever, thy missiles were terrible: from these surely exempt us!

Destroy the fever that returns on each third day, the one that intermits each third day, the one that continues without intermission, and the autumnal one; destroy the cold fever, the hot, him that comes in summer, and him that arrives in the rainy season![2]

(5.22)

[a] Perhaps the fever as diarrhea maker.

[b] This and following names are designations of peoples located outside of the Aryan area of India.

3. *A Prayer for Success in Gambling*

The successful, victorious, skilfully gaming Apsarā,[a] that Apsarā who makes the winnings in the game of dice, do I call hither.

The skilfully gaming Apsarā who sweeps and heaps up the stakes, that Apsarā who takes the winnings in the game of dice, do I call hither.

May she, who dances about with the dice, when she takes the stakes from the game of dice, when she desires to win for us, obtain the advantage by her magic! May she come to us full of abundance! Let them not win this wealth of ours!

The Apsarās who rejoice in dice, who carry grief and wrath —that joyful and exulting Apsarā, do I call hither.[2]

(4.38)

[a] A female Divinity, the Indian "nymph."

4. *The Pearl and Its Shell as an Amulet*

Born of the wind, the atmosphere, the lightning, and the light, may this pearl shell, born of gold, protect us from straits!

With the shell which was born in the sea, at the head of bright substances, we slay the Rakṣas[a] and conquer the Atrins.[b]

With the shell we conquer disease and poverty; with the shell, too, the Sadānvās.[c] The shell is our universal remedy; the pearl shall protect us from straits!

Born in the heavens, born in the sea, brought on from the river, this shell, born of gold, is our life-prolonging amulet.

The amulet, born from the sea, a sun, born from the cloud, shall on all sides protect us from the missiles of the gods and the Asuras!

Thou art one of the golden substances, thou art born from the moon. Thou art sightly on the chariot, thou art brilliant on the quiver.

The bone of the gods turned into pearl; that, animated, dwells in the waters. That do I fasten upon thee unto life, lustre, strength, longevity, unto a life lasting a hundred autumns. May the amulet of pearl protect thee![2]

(4.10)

[a] A class of demons.
[b] Devouring demons.
[c] Female demons.

5. *Charm to Arouse the Passionate Love of a Woman*

May love, the disquieter, disquiet thee; do not hold out upon thy bed! With the terrible arrow of Kāma[a] do I pierce thee in the heart.

The arrow, winged with longing, barbed with love, whose shaft is undeviating desire, with that, well-aimed, Kāma shall pierce thee in the heart!

With that well-aimed arrow of Kāma which parches the spleen, whose plume flies forward, which burns up, do I pierce thee in the heart.

Consumed by burning ardour, with parched mouth, do thou, woman, come to me, thy pride laid aside, mine alone, speaking sweetly and to me devoted!

I drive thee with a goad from thy mother and thy father, so that thou shalt be in my power, shalt come up to my wish.

All her thoughts do ye, O Mitra and Varuṇa,[b] drive out of her! Then, having deprived her of her will, put her into my power alone![2]

(3.25)

[a] The god of love.
[b] Two powerful Ṛg-vedic gods.

6. *Expiation for the Irregular Appearance of the First Pair of Teeth*

These two teeth, the tigers, that have broken forth, eager to devour father and mother, do thou, O Brahmaṇaspati Jātavedas,[a] render auspicious!

Do ye eat rice, eat barley, and eat, too beans, as well as sesamum! That, O teeth, is the share deposited for your enrichment. Do not injure father and mother!

Since ye have been invoked, O teeth, be ye in unison kind and propitious! Elsewhere, O teeth, shall pass away the fierce qualities of your body! Do not injure father and mother![2]

(6.140)

[a] Two Ṛg-vedic gods (Bṛhaspati and Agni).

7. *Charm to Stop the Flow of Blood*

The maidens that go yonder, the veins, clothed in red garments, like sisters without a brother, bereft of strength, they shall stand still!

Stand still, thou lower one, stand still, thou higher one; do thou in the middle also stand still! The most tiny vein stands still: may then the great artery also stand still!

Of the hundred arteries, and the thousand veins, those in the middle here have indeed stood still. At the same time the ends have ceased to flow.

Around you has passed a great sandy dike:[a] stand ye still, pray take your ease![2]

(1.17)

[a] Perhaps an application of sand put upon or about the wound.

8. *Hymn to Goddess Earth*

Truth, greatness, universal order, strength, consecration, creative fervour, spiritual exaltation, the sacrifice, support the earth. May this earth, the mistress of that which was and shall be, prepare for us a broad domain!

The earth that has heights, and slopes, and great plains, that supports the plants of manifold virtue, free from the pressure that comes from the midst of men, she shall spread out for us, and fit herself for us!

The earth upon which the sea, and the rivers and the waters, upon which food and the tribes of men have arisen, upon which this breathing, moving life exists, shall afford us precedence in drinking!

The earth whose are the four regions of space, upon which food and the tribes of men have arisen, which supports the manifold breathing, moving things, shall afford us cattle and other possessions also!

The earth upon which of old the first men unfolded themselves, upon which the gods overcame the Asuras,[a] shall procure for us all kinds of cattle, horse, and fowls, good fortune, and glory!

The earth that supports all, furnishes wealth, the foundation, the golden-breasted resting-place of all living creatures, she that supports Agni Vaiśvānara,[b] and mates with Indra, the bull, shall furnish us with property!

The broad earth, which the sleepless gods ever attentively guard, shall milk for us precious honey, and, moreover, besprinkle us with glory!

That earth which formerly was water upon the ocean of space, which the seers found out by their skilful devices; whose heart is in the highest heaven, immortal, surrounded by truth, shall bestow upon us brilliancy and strength, and place us in supreme sovereignty!

That earth upon which the attendant waters jointly flow by day and night unceasingly, shall pour out milk for us in rich streams, and, moreover, besprinkle us with glory!

The earth which the Aśvins have measured, upon which Viṣṇu has stepped out, which Indra, the lord of might, has made friendly to himself; she, the mother, shall pour forth milk for me, the son!

Thy snowy mountain heights, and thy forests, O earth, shall be kind to us! The brown, the black, the red, the multicoloured, the firm earth, that is protected by Indra, I have settled upon, not suppressed, not slain, not wounded.

Into thy middle set us, O earth, and into thy navel, into the nourishing strength that has grown up from thy body; purify thyself for us! The earth is the mother, and I the son of the earth; Parjanya[c] is the father; he, too, shall save us!

The earth upon which the priests inclose the altar, upon which they, devoted to all holy works, unfold the sacrifice, upon which are set up, in front of the sacrifice, the sacrificial posts, erect and brilliant, that earth shall prosper us, herself prospering!

Him that hates us, O earth, him that battles against us, him that is hostile towards us with his mind and his weapons, do thou subject to us, anticipating our wish by deed!

The mortals born of thee live on thee, thou supportest both bipeds and quadrupeds. Thine, O earth, are these five races of men, the mortals, upon whom the rising sun sheds undying light with his rays.

These creatures all together shall yield milk for us; do thou, O earth, give us the honey of speech!

Upon the firm, broad earth, the all-begetting mother of the plants, that is supported by divine law, upon her, propitious and kind, may we ever pass our lives!

A great gathering-place thou, great earth, hast become; great haste, commotion, and agitation are upon thee. Great Indra protects thee unceasingly. Do thou, O earth, cause us to brighten as if at the sight of gold: not any one shall hate us!

Upon the earth men give to the gods the sacrifice, the prepared oblation; upon the earth mortal men live pleasantly by food. May this earth give us breath and life, may she cause me to reach old age!

The fragrance, O earth, that has arisen upon thee, which the plants and the waters hold, which the Gandharvas and the Apsarās[d] have partaken of, with that make me fragrant: not any one shall hate us!

That fragrance of thine which has entered into the lotus, that fragrance, O earth, which the immortals of yore gathered up at the marriage of Sūryā,[e] with that make me fragrant: not any one shall hate us!

That fragrance of thine which is in men, the loveliness and charm that is in male and female, that which is in steeds and heroes, that which is in the wild animals with trunks, the lustre that is in the maiden, O earth, with that do thou blend us: not any one shall hate us!

Rock, stone, dust is this earth; this earth is supported, held together. To this golden-breasted earth I have rendered obeisance.

The earth, upon whom the forest-sprung trees ever stand firm, the all-nourishing, compact earth, do we invoke.

Rising or sitting, standing or walking, may we not stumble with our right or left foot upon the earth!

To the pure earth I speak, to the ground, the soil that has grown through the spiritual exaltation. Upon thee, that holdest nourishment, prosperity, food, and ghee, we would settle down, O earth!

Purified the waters shall flow for our bodies; what flows off from us that do we deposit upon him we dislike: with a purifier, O earth, do I purify myself!

Thy easterly regions, and thy northern, thy southerly regions, O earth, and thy western, shall be kind to me as I walk upon thee! May I that have been placed into the world not fall down!

Do not drive us from the west, nor from the east; not from the north, and not from the south! Security be thou for us, O earth: waylayers shall not find us, hold far away their murderous weapon!

As long as I look out upon thee, O earth, with the sun as my companion, so long shall my sight not fail, as year followeth upon year!

When, as I lie, I turn upon my right or left side, O earth; when stretched out we lie with our ribs upon thee pressing against us, do not, O earth, that liest close to everything, there injure us!

What, O earth, I dig out of thee, quickly shall that grow again: may I not, O pure one, pierce thy vital spot, and not thy heart!

Thy summer, O earth, thy rainy season, thy autumn, winter, early spring, and spring; thy decreed yearly seasons, thy days and nights shall yield us milk!

The pure earth that starts in fright away from the serpent, upon whom were the fires that are within the waters, she that delivers to destruction the blasphemous Dasyus,[f] she that takes the side of god Indra, not of Vr̥tra,[g] that earth adheres to the mighty god, the lusty bull.

Upon whom rests the sacrificial hut and the two vehicles that hold the *soma*, in whom the sacrificial post is fixed, upon whom the Brâhmanas praise the gods with *r̥cs* and *sāmans*, knowing also the *yajus*-formulas;[g] upon whom the serving-priests are employed so that Indra shall drink the *soma*;—

Upon whom the seers of yore, that created the beings,

brought forth with their songs the cows, they the seven active priests, by means of the offerings, the sacrifices, and their creative fervour;—

May this earth point out to us the wealth that we crave; may Fortune add his help, may Indra come here as our champion!

The earth upon whom the noisy mortals sing and dance, upon whom they fight, upon whom resounds the roaring drum, shall drive forth our enemies, shall make us free from rivals!

To the earth upon whom are food, and rice and barley, upon whom live these five races of men, to the earth, the wife of Parjanya, that is fattened by rain, be reverence!

The earth upon whose ground the citadels constructed by the gods unfold themselves, every region of her that is the womb of all, Prajāpati,[h] shall make pleasant for us!

The earth that holds treasures manifold in secret places, wealth, jewels, and gold shall she give to me; she that bestows wealth liberally, the kindly goddess, wealth shall she bestow upon us!

The earth that holds people of manifold varied speech, of different customs, according to their habitations, as a reliable milch-cow that does not kick, shall she milk for me a thousand streams of wealth!

The serpent, the scorpion with thirsty fangs, that hibernating torpidly lies upon thee; the worm, and whatever living thing, O earth, moves in the rainy season, shall, when it creeps, not creep upon us: with what is auspicious on thee be gracious to us!

Thy many paths upon which people go, thy tracks for chariots and wagons to advance upon which both good and evil proceed, this road, free from enemies, and free from thieves, may we gain: with what is auspicious on thee be gracious to us!

The earth holds the fool and holds the wise, endures that good and bad dwell upon her; she keeps company with the boar, gives herself up to the wild hog.

Thy forest animals, the wild animals homed in the woods, the man-eating lions, and tigers that roam; the wolf, mishap, injury, and demons, O earth, drive away from us!

The earth upon whom the biped birds fly together, the flamingoes, eagles, birds of prey, and fowls; upon whom the wind hastens, raising the dust, and tossing the trees—as the wind blows forth and back the flame bursts after;—

The earth upon whom day and night jointly, black and bright, have been decreed, the broad earth covered and enveloped with rain, shall kindly place us into every pleasant abode!

O mother earth, kindly set me down upon a well-founded place! With father heaven cooperating, O thou wise one, do thou place me into happiness and prosperity![2]

(12.1)

[a] The opponents of the gods.
[b] Fire god as "relating to all men."
[c] God of rain.
[d] Male and female divinities.
[e] The wife of Sūryā, or the Sun.
[f] Demons.
[g] Indra's enemy.
[h] A supreme god.

III. The *Śatapatha-Brāhmaṇa*

The *Brāhmaṇa* (or Brahmanical exegesis) *of the Hundred Paths* is the first great work of Vedic literature written in prose. Tentatively it may be placed in the tenth century B.C. As in all the texts of the same class, discussions on sacred formulas (*mantras*) or doctrinal points concerning sacrifice are to be found along with mythological ramblings and erudite or allegorical digressions. The *Śatapatha* contains the oldest speculation on *brāhman,* or the Absolute Principle (see, for instance, No. 2 below).

1. *Death and the Gods*

The year, doubtless, is the same as death, for Father Time it is who, by means of day and night, destroys the life of mortal beings, and then they die: therefore the year is the same as death; and whosoever knows this year to be death, his life that year does not destroy, by day and night, before old age, and he attains his full extent of life.

And he, indeed, is the Ender, for it is he who, by day and night, reaches the end of the life of mortals, and then they die: therefore he is the Ender, and whosoever knows this year, death, the Ender, the end of his life that year does not reach, by day and night, before old age, and he attains his full extent of life.

The gods were afraid of this Prajāpati, the year, death, the Ender, lest he, by day and night, should reach the end of their life.

They performed these sacrificial rites—the Agnihotra,[a] the New and Full-moon sacrifices, the Seasonal offerings, the animal sacrifice, and the Soma-sacrifice: by offering these sacrifices they did not attain immortality.

They also built a fire-altar,—they laid down unlimited enclosing-stones, unlimited *yajuṣmatī*[b] bricks, unlimited *lokampṛṇā*[c] bricks, even as some lay them down to this day, saying, "The gods did so." They did not attain immortality.

They went on praising and toiling, striving to win immortality. Prajāpati then spake unto them, "Ye do not lay down all my forms; but ye either make me too large or leave me defective: therefore ye do not become immortal."

They spake, "Tell thou us thyself, then, in what manner we may lay down all thy forms!"

He spake, "Lay ye down three hundred and sixty enclosing-stones, three hundred and sixty *yajuṣmatī* bricks, and thirty-six thereunto; and of *lokampṛṇā* bricks lay ye down ten thousand and eight hundred; and ye will be laying down all my forms, and will become immortal." And the gods laid down accordingly, and thereafter became immortal.

Death spake unto the gods, "Surely, on this wise all men will become immortal, and what share will then be mine?" They spake, "Henceforward no one shall be immortal with the body: only when thou shalt have taken that body as thy share, he who is to become immortal either through knowledge, or through holy work, shall become immortal after separating from the body." Now when they said "either through knowledge, or through holy work," it is this fire-altar that is the knowledge, and this fire-altar that is the holy work.

And they who so know this, or they who do this holy work, come to life again when they have died, and, coming to life, they come to immortal life. But they who do not know this, or do not do this holy work, come to life again when they die, and they become the food of Death time after time.[3]

(10.4, 3)

[a] Name of the daily oblation to god Agni.
[b] Literally, "accompanied by a sacrificial formula."
[c] Literally, "filling the world."

2. *The Brāhman*

Let him meditate upon the "true *brāhman*." Now, man here, indeed, is possessed of understanding, and according to how great his understanding is when he departs this world, so does he, on passing away, enter yonder world.

Let him meditate on the Self, which is made up of intelligence, and endowed with a body of spirit, with a form of light, and with an etherial nature, which changes its shape at will, is swift as thought, of true resolve, and true purpose, which consists of all sweet odours and tastes, which holds sway over all the regions and pervades this whole universe, which is speechless and indifferent;—even as a grain of rice, or a grain of barley, or a grain of millet, or the smallest granule of millet, so is this golden Puruṣa in the heart; even as a smokeless light, it is greater than the sky, greater than the ether, greater than the earth, greater than all existing things; —that self of the spirit is my self; on passing away from hence I shall obtain that self. Verily, whosoever has this trust, for him there is no uncertainty.

Thus spake Śāṇḍilya,[a] and so it is.[3]

(10.6, 3, 1–2)

[a] Name of a celebrated teacher.

3. *The Indian Legend of the Deluge*

In the morning they brought to Manu[a] water for washing, just as now also they are wont to bring water for washing the hands. When he was washing himself, a fish came into his hands.

It spake to him the word, "Rear me, I will save thee!" "Wherefrom wilt thou save me?" "A flood will carry away all these creatures: from that I will save thee!" "How am I to rear thee?"

It said, "As long as we are small, there is great destruction for us: fish devours fish. Thou wilt first keep me in a jar. When I outgrow that, thou wilt dig a pit and keep me in it. When I outgrow that, thou wilt take me down the sea, for then I shall be beyond destruction."

It soon became a large fish. Thereupon it said, "In such and such a year that flood will come. Thou shalt then attend to my advice by preparing a ship; and when the flood has risen thou shalt enter into the ship, and I will save thee from it."

After he had reared it in this way, he took it down to the sea. And in the same year which the fish had indicated to him, he attended to the advice of the fish by preparing a ship; and when the flood had risen, he entered into the ship. The fish then swam up to him, and to its horn he tied the rope of the ship, and by that means he passed swiftly up to yonder northern mountain.

It then said, "I have saved thee. Fasten the ship to a tree;

but let not the water cut thee off, whilst thou art on the mountain. As the water subsides, thou mayest gradually descend!" Accordingly he gradually descended, and hence that slope of the northern mountain is called "Manu's descent!" The flood then swept away all these creatures, and Manu alone remained here.[a]

(1.8,1, 1–6)

[a] The father of the human race.

4. *Cosmogony*

Verily, in the beginning this universe was water, nothing but a sea of water. The waters desired, "How can we be reproduced?" They toiled and performed fervid devotions, when they were becoming heated, a golden egg was produced. The year, indeed, was not then in existence: this golden egg floated about for as long as the space of a year.

In a year's time a man, this Prajāpati,[a] was produced therefrom; and hence a woman, a cow, or a mare brings forth within the space of a year; for Prajāpati was born in a year. He broke open this golden egg. There was then, indeed, no resting-place; only this golden egg, bearing him, floated about for as long as the space of a year.

At the end of a year he tried to speak. He said "bhūḥr": this word became this earth;—"bhuvar": this became this air;—"svar": this became yonder sky. Therefore a child tries to speak at the end of a year, for at the end of a year Prajāpati tried to speak.

When he was first speaking, Prajāpati spoke words of one syllable and of two syllables; whence a child, when first speaking, speaks words of one syllable and of two syllables.

These three words consist of five syllables: he made them to be the five seasons. At the end of the first year, Prajāpati rose to stand on these words thus produced; whence a child tries to stand up at the end of a year, for at the end of a year Prajāpati stood up.

He was born with a life of a thousand years: even as one

might see in the distance the opposite shore, so did he behold the opposite shore of his own life.

Desirous of offspring, he went on singing praises and toiling. He laid the power of reproduction into his own self. By the breath of his mouth he created the gods: the gods were created on entering the sky; and this is the godhead of the gods that they were created on entering the sky. Having created them, there was, as it were, daylight for him; and this also is the godhead of the gods that, after creating them, there was, as it were, daylight for him.

And by the downward breathing he created the Asuras:[b] they were created on entering this earth. Having created them there was, as it were, darkness for him.

Now what daylight, as it were, there was for him, on creating the gods, of that he made the day; and what darkness, as it were, there was for him, on creating the Asuras, of that he made the night: they are these two, day and night.[3]

(11.1, 6, 1–11)

[a] "Lord of creatures," the supreme god to come.
[b] A class of demons, opponents of the gods.

IV. The *Upaniṣads*

The *Upaniṣads* or "Approaches" are collections of texts developing the ritual or cosmogonic data of the Veda in a strongly speculative direction and installing on new foundations the ancient equivalence felt between the human and the divine world. They mark the "end of the Veda," that is to say, that point of completion of Vedic representations which was foreshadowed by the assumed identity between the *ātman*, or "individual soul," and the *brāhman*, or "universal soul." The teaching is imparted in discursive form with the help of parables, dialogues, maxims, inspired in form by the old *Brāhmaṇas*. The two principal *Upaniṣads* are the so-called "*Great Āraṇyaka*" and the *Chāndogya;* they could be dated from the sixth century B.C.

No. 1 below (Īśā) develops disjointed ideas on the theme of unity in diversity, on the all-surpassing paradoxical world-being, on the necessity of transcending the antithesis of knowing and of being, etc.

The dialogue between the Master Yājñavalkya and his wife Maitreyī (in No. 4) concerns the Universal Soul.

No. 7 is the Indian replica of the famous apologue of Limbs and Stomach.

By means of an allegory, No. 8 shows how *brāhman* is superior to all the gods (Fire, Wind, Indra) who try in vain to control it and in reality do not know its greatness. The knowledge of *brāhman* is intuitive: it resembles the cry of astonishment which follows a sudden appearance of lightning, or rather a memory which passes across the mind.

In No. 9, a dying father leaves his limbs and powers to his son; on receiving the gift, the son is identified with his father, who, sacrificed (in the literal sense), immediately finds access to the divine world.

1. *Unity and Diversity*

By the Lord enveloped must this all be—
Whatever moving thing there is in the moving
  world.
With this renounced, thou mayest enjoy.
Covet not the wealth of anyone at all.

Even while doing deeds here,
One may desire to live a hundred years.
Thus on thee—not otherwise than this is it—
The dead adheres not on the man.

Devilish are those worlds called,
With blind darkness covered o'er!
Unto them, on deceasing, go
Whatever folk are slayers of the Self.

Unmoving, the One[a] is swifter than the mind.
The sense-powers reached not It, speeding on
before.
Past others running, This goes standing.
In It Mātariśvan[b] places action.

It moves. It moves not.
It is far, and It is near.
It is within all this,
And It is outside of all this.

Now, he who on all beings
Looks as just in the Self,
And on the Self as in all beings—
He does not shrink away from Him.

In whom all beings
Have become just the Self of the discerner—
Then what delusion, what sorrow is there,
Of him who perceives the unity!

Into blind darkness enter they
That worship ignorance;
Into darkness greater than that, as it were, they
That delight in knowledge.

Knowledge and non-knowledge—
He who this pair conjointly knows,
With non-knowledge passing over death,
With knowledge wins the immortal.

Into blind darkness enter they
Who worship non-becoming;
Into darkness greater than that, as it were, they
Who delight in becoming.

Becoming and destruction—
He who this pair conjointly knows,
With destruction passing over death,
With becoming wins the immortal.[4]

(*Īśā*)

[a] The Absolute (as a neuter form).
[b] The god of the wind.

2. *The Unitary World-Soul*

As the one fire has entered the world
And becomes corresponding in form to every form,
So the one Inner Soul of all things
Is corresponding in form to every form, and yet is
outside.

As the one wind has entered the world
And becomes corresponding in form to every form,
So the one Inner Soul of all things
Is corresponding in form to every form, and yet is
outside.

As the sun, the eye of the whole world,
Is not sullied by the external faults of the eyes,
So the one Inner Soul of all things
Is not sullied by the evil in the world, being external
to it.

The Inner Soul of all things, the One Controller,
Who makes his one form manifold—
The wise who perceive Him as standing in oneself,
They, and no others, have eternal happiness!

Him who is the Constant among the inconstant, the
 Intelligent among intelligences,
The One among many, who grants desires—
The wise who perceive Him as standing in oneself,
They, and no others, have eternal peace![4]

(*Kaṭha*, 5.9–13)

3. *The Creation of the World from the Soul*

In the beginning this world was Soul alone in the form of a Person. Looking around, he saw nothing else than himself. He said first: "I am." Thence arose the name "I." Therefore even today, when one is addressed, he says first just "It is I" and then speaks whatever name he has. Since before all this world he burned up all evils, therefore he is a person. He who knows this, verily, burns up him who desires to be ahead of him.

He was afraid. Therefore one who is alone is afraid. This one then thought to himself: "Since there is nothing else than myself, of what am I afraid?" Thereupon, verily, his fear departed, for of what should he have been afraid? Assuredly it is from a second that fear arises.

Verily, he had no delight. Therefore one alone has no delight. He desired a second. He was, indeed, as large as a woman and a man closely embraced. He caused that self to fall into two pieces. Therefrom arose a husband and a wife. Therefore this is true: "Oneself is like a half-fragment," as Yājñavalkya used to say. Therefore this space is filled by a wife. He copulated with her. Therefrom human beings were produced.

And she then bethought herself: "How now does he copulate with me after he has produced me just from himself? Come, let me hide myself." She became a cow. He became a bull. With her he did indeed copulate. Then cattle were born. She became a mare, he a stallion. She became a female ass, he a male ass; with her he copulated, of a truth. Thence were born solid-hoofed animals. She became a she-goat, he a he-goat; she a ewe, he a ram. With her he did verily copulate. Therefrom were born goats and sheep. Thus, indeed, he created all, whatever pairs there are, even down to the ants.

He knew: "I, indeed, am this creation, for I emitted it all from myself." Thence arose creation. Verily, he who has this knowledge comes to be in that creation of his.

Then he rubbed thus. From his mouth as the fire-hole and from his hands he created fire. Both the hands and the mouth are hairless on the inside, for the fire-hole is hairless on the inside.

This that people say, "Worship this god! Worship that god!"—one god after another—this is his creation indeed! And he himself is all the gods.

Now, whatever is moist, that he created from semen, and that is Soma. This whole world, verily, is just food and the eater of food.

That was Brahman's super-creation: namely, that he created the gods, his superiors; likewise, that, being mortal, he created the immortals. Therefore was it a super-creation. Verily, he who knows this comes to be in that super-creation of his.

Verily, at that time the world was undifferentiated. It became differentiated just by name and form, as the saying is: "He has such a name, such a form." Even today this world is differentiated just by name and form, as the saying is: "He has such a name, such a form."

He entered in here, even to the fingernail-tips, as a razor would be hidden in a razor-case, or fire in a fire-holder. Him they see not, for as seen he is incomplete. When breathing, he becomes breath by name; when speaking, the voice; when seeing, the eye; when hearing, the ear; when thinking, the mind: these are merely the names of his acts. Whoever worships one or another of these—he knows not; for he is incomplete with one or another of these. One should worship with the thought that he is just one's self, for therein all these become one. That same thing, namely this self, is the trace of this All, for by it one knows this All. Just as, verily, one might find by a footprint, thus. He finds fame and praise who knows this.

That Self is dearer than a son, is dearer than wealth, is dearer than all else, since this self is nearer.

If of one who speaks of anything else than the Self as dear, one should say, "He will lose what he holds dear," he would indeed be likely to do so. One should reverence the Self alone as dear. He who reverences the Self alone as dear—what he holds dear, verily, is not perishable.[4]

(*Bṛhad-Āraṇyaka,* 1.4, 1–8)

4. *The Conversation between Yājñavalkya and Maitreyī*

"Maitreyī!" said Yājñavalkya, "lo, verily, I am about to go forth from this state. Behold! let me make a final settlement for you and that Kātyāyanī."

Then said Maitreyī: "If now, sir, this whole earth filled with wealth were mine, would I be immortal thereby?"

"No," said Yājñavalkya. "As the life of the rich, even so would your life be. Of immortality, however, there is no hope through wealth."

Then said Maitreyī: "What should I do with that through which I may not be immortal? What you know, sir—that, indeed, tell me!"

Then said Yājñavalkya: "Ah! Lo, dear as you are to us, dear is what you say! Come, sit down. I will explain to you. But while I am expounding, do you seek to ponder thereon."

Then said he: "Lo, verily, not for love of the husband is a husband dear, but for love of the Soul a husband is dear.

"Lo, verily, not for love of the wife is a wife dear, but for love of the Soul a wife is dear.

"Lo, verily, not for love of the sons are sons dear, but for love of the Souls sons are dear.

"Lo, verily, not for love of wealth is wealth dear, but for love of the Soul wealth is dear.

"Lo, verily, not for love of Brahmanhood is Brahmanhood dear, but for love of the Soul Brahmanhood is dear.

"Lo, verily, not for love of the worlds are the worlds dear, but for love of the Soul the worlds are dear.

"Lo, verily, not for the love of the gods are the gods dear, but for love of the Soul the gods are dear.

"Lo, verily, not for love of beings are beings dear, but for love of the Soul beings are dear.

"Lo, verily, not for love of all is all dear, but for love of the Soul all is dear.

"Lo, verily, it is the Soul that should be seen, that should be hearkened to, that should be thought on, that should be pondered on, O Maitreyī. Lo, verily, with the seeing of, with the hearkening to, with the thinking of, and with the understanding of the Soul, this world-all is known.

"Brahmanhood has deserted him who knows Brahmanhood in aught else than the Soul.

"The worlds have deserted him who knows the worlds in aught else than the Soul.

"The gods have deserted him who knows the gods in aught else than the Soul.

"Beings have deserted him who knows beings in aught else than the Soul.

"Everything has deserted him who knows everything in aught else than the Soul.

"It is—as, when a drum is being beaten, one would not be able to grasp the external sounds, but by grasping the drum or the beater of the drum the sound is grasped.

"It is—as, when a conch-shell is being blown, one would not be able to grasp the external sounds, but by grasping the drum or the beater of the drum the sound is grasped.

"It is—as, when a lute is being played, one would not be able to grasp the external sounds, but by grasping the lute or the player of the lute the sound is grasped.

"It is—as, from a fire laid with damp fuel, clouds of smoke separately issue forth, so, lo, verily, from this great Being has been breathed forth that which is *Ṛg-Veda, Yajur-Veda, Sāma-Veda,* Hymns of the Atharvans and Aṅgiras', Legend, Ancient Lore, Sciences, Mystic Doctrines, Verses, Aphorisms,

Explanations, and Commentaries. From it, indeed, are all these breathed forth.

"It is—as of all waters the uniting-point is the sea, so of all touches the uniting-point is the skin, so of all tastes the uniting-point is the tongue, so of all smells the uniting-point is the nostrils, so of all forms the uniting-point is the eye, so of all sounds the uniting-point is the ear, so of all intentions the uniting-point is the mind, so of all knowledges the uniting-point is the heart, so of all acts the uniting-point is the hands, so of all pleasures the uniting-point is the generative organ, so of all evacuations the uniting-point is the anus, so of all journeys the uniting-point is the feet, so of all the Vedas the uniting-point is speech.

"It is—as a lump of salt cast in water would dissolve right into the water; there would not be any of it to seize forth, as it were, but wherever one may take, it is salty indeed—so, lo, verily, this great Being, infinite, limitless, is just a mass of knowledge.

"Arising out of these elements, into them also one vanishes away. After death there is no consciousness. Thus, lo, say I." Thus spake Yājñavalkya.

Then spake Maitreyī: "Herein, indeed, you have bewildered me, sir—in saying: "After death there is no consciousness!"

Then spake Yājñavalkya: "Lo, verily, I speak not bewilderment. Sufficient, lo, verily is this for understanding.

"For where there is a duality, as it were, there one sees another; there one smells another; there one hears another; there one speaks to another; there one thinks of another; there one understands another. Where, verily, everything has become just one's own self, then whereby and whom would one smell? then whereby and whom would one see? then whereby and whom would one hear? then whereby and to whom would one speak? then whereby and on whom would one think? then whereby and whom would one understand? Whereby would one understand him by whom one understands this All? Lo, whereby would one understand the understander?"[4]

(*Ibid.*, 2.4)

5. *The Soul in Dreamless Sleep*

"As a falcon, or an eagle, having flown around here in space, becomes weary, folds its wings, and is borne down to its nest, just so this person hastens to that state where, asleep, he desires no desires and sees no dream.

"Verily, a person has those channels called hitā; as a hair subdivided a thousandfold, so minute are they, full of white, blue, yellow, green, and red. Now when people seem to be killing him, when they seem to be overpowering him, when an elephant seems to be tearing him to pieces, when he seems to be falling into a hole—in these circumstances he is imagining through ignorance the very fear which he sees when awake. When, imagining that he is a god, that he is a king, he thinks 'I am this world-all,' that is his highest world.

"This, verily, is that form of his which is beyond desires, free from evil, without fear. As a man, when in the embrace of a beloved wife, knows nothing within or without, so this person, when in the embrace of the intelligent Soul, knows nothing within or without. Verily, that is his true form in which his desire is satisfied, in which the Soul is his desire, in which he is without desire and without sorrow.

"There a father becomes not a father; a mother, not a mother; the worlds, not the worlds; the gods, not the gods; the Vedas, not the Vedas; a thief, not a thief. He is not followed by good, he is not followed by evil, for then he has passed beyond all sorrows of the heart.

"An ocean, a seer alone without duality, becomes he whose world is Brahman, O King!"—thus Yājñavalkya instructed him. "This is a man's highest path. This is his highest achievement. This is his highest world. This is his highest bliss. On a part of just this bliss other creatures have their living.

"If one is fortunate among men and wealthy, lord over others, best provided with all human enjoyments—that is the highest bliss of men. Now a hundredfold the bliss of men is one bliss of those who have won the fathers' world. Now a hundredfold the bliss of those who have won the fathers' world is one bliss in the Gandharva-world. A hundredfold the bliss in the Gandharva-world is one bliss of the gods who gain their divinity by meritorious works. A hundredfold the bliss of the gods by works is one bliss of the gods by birth and of him who is learned in the Vedas, who is without crookedness, and who is free from desire. A hundredfold the bliss of the gods by birth is one bliss in the Prajāpati-world and of him who is learned in the Vedas, who is without crookedness, and is free from desire. A hundredfold the bliss in the Prajāpati-world is one bliss in the Brahman-world and of him who is learned in the Vedas, who is without crookedness, and who is free from desire. This truly is the highest world. This is the Brahman-world, O King."—Thus spake Yājñavalkya.[4]

(*Ibid.*, 4.3, 19–33, *passim*)

6. *The Individual Soul Identical with Brahman*

Verily, this whole world is *Brahman*. Tranquil, let one worship It as from which he came forth, as that into which he will be dissolved, as that in which he breathes.

Now, verily, a person consists of purpose. According to the purpose which a person has in this world, thus does he become on departing hence. So let him form for himself a purpose.

He who consists of mind, whose body is life, whose form is light, whose conception is truth, whose soul is space, containing all works, containing all desires, containing all odors, containing all tastes, encompassing this whole world, the unspeaking, the unconcerned—this Soul of mine within the heart is smaller than a grain of rice, or a barley-corn, or a mustard-seed, or a grain of millet, or the kernel of a grain of millet; this Soul of mine within the heart is greater than the earth, greater than the atmosphere, greater than the sky, greater than these worlds.

Containing all works, containing all desires, containing all odors, containing all tastes, encompassing this whole world, the unspeaking, the unconcerned—this is the Soul of mine within the heart, this is *Brahman*. Into him I shall enter on departing hence.

If one would believe this, he would have no more doubt.— Thus used Śāṇḍilya to say—yea, Śāṇḍilya![4]

(*Chandogya*, 3.14)

7. *The Rivalry of the Five Bodily Functions, and the Superiority of Breath*

Om! Verily, he who knows the chiefest and best, becomes the chiefest and best. Breath, verily, is the chiefest and best.

Verily, he who knows the most excellent, becomes the most excellent of his own people. Speech, verily, is the most excellent.

Verily, he who knows the firm basis, has a firm basis both in this world and in the yonder. The eye, verily, is a firm basis.

Verily, he who knows attainment—for him wishes are attained, both human and divine. The ear, verily, is attainment.

Verily, he who knows attainment—for him wishes are attained, both human and divine. The ear, verily, is attainment.

Verily, he who knows the abode, becomes an abode of his own people. The mind, verily, is the abode.

Now, the Vital Breaths disputed among themselves on self-superiority, saying in turn: "I am superior!" "I am superior!"

Those Vital Breaths went to Father Prajāpati, and said: "Sir! Which of us is the most superior?"

He said to them: "That one of you after whose going off the body appears as if it were the very worst off—he is the most superior of you."

Speech went off. Having remained away a year, it came around again, and said: "How have you been able to live without me?"

"As the dumb, not speaking, but breathing with the breath, seeing with the eye, hearing with the ear, thinking with the mind. Thus."

Speech entered in.

The Eye went off. Having remained away a year, it came

around again, and said: "How have you been able to live without me?"

"As the blind, not seeing, but breathing with the breath, speaking with speech, hearing with the ear, thinking with the mind. Thus."

The Eye entered in.

The Ear went off. Having remained away a year, it came around again, and said: "How have you been able to live without me?"

"As the deaf, not hearing, but breathing with the breath, speaking with speech, seeing with the eye, thinking with the mind. Thus."

The Ear entered in.

The Mind went off. Having remained away a year, it came around again, and said: "How have you been able to live without me?"

"As simpletons, mindless, but breathing with the breath, speaking with speech, seeing with the eye, hearing with the ear. Thus."

The mind entered in.

Now when the Breath was about to go off—as a fine horse might tear out the pegs of his foot-tethers all together, thus did it tear out the other Breaths all together. They all came to it and said: "Sir! Remain. You are the most superior of us. Do not go off."

The Speech said unto that one: "If I am the most excellent, so are you the most excellent."

Then the Eye said unto that one: "If I am a firm basis, so are you a firm basis."

Then the Ear said unto that one: "If I am attainment, so are you attainment."

Then the Mind said unto that one: "If I am an abode, so are you an abode."

Verily, they do not call them "Speeches," nor "Eyes," nor "Ears," nor "Minds." They call them "Breaths," for the vital breath is all these.[4]

(*Ibid.,* 5.1)

8. *Allegory of the Vedic Gods' Ignorance of Brahman*

Now, Brahman won a victory for the gods. Now, in the victory of this Brahman the gods were exulting. They bethought themselves: "Ours indeed is this victory! Ours indeed is this greatness!"

Now, Brahman understood this of them. It appeared to them. They did not understand it. "What wonderful being is this?" they said.

They said to Fire: "All-possessor, find out this—what this wonderful being is."

"So be it."

He ran unto It.

Unto him It spoke: "Who are you?"

"Verily, I am Fire," he said. "Verily, I am All-possessor."

"In such as you what power is there?"

"Indeed, I might burn everything here, whatever there is here in the earth!"

It put down a straw before him. "Burn that!"

He went forth at it with all speed. He was not able to burn it. Thereupon indeed he returned, saying: "I have not been able to find out this—what this wonderful being is."

Then they said to Wind: "Wind, find out this—what this wonderful being is."

"So be it."

He ran unto It.

Unto him It spoke: "Who are you?"

"Verily, I am Wind," he said. "Verily, I am Mātariśvan."

"In such as you what power is there?"

"Indeed, I might carry off everything here, whatever there is here in the earth."

It put down a straw before him. "Carry that off!"

He went at it with all speed. He was not able to carry it off. Thereupon indeed he returned, saying: "I have not been able to find out this—what this wonderful being is."

Then they said to Indra: "O Liberal, find out this—what this wonderful being is."

"So be it."

He ran unto It. It disappeared from him.

In that very space he came upon a woman exceedingly beautiful, Umā, daughter of the Snowy Mountain.

To her he said: "What is this wonderful being?"

"It is Brahman," she said. "In that victory of Brahman, verily, exult ye."

Thereupon he knew it was Brahman.

Therefore, verily, these gods, namely Fire, Wind, and Indra, are above the other gods, as it were; for these touched It nearest, for these and specially Indra first knew It was Brahman.

Therefore, verily, Indra is above the other gods, as it were; for he touched It nearest, for he first knew It was Brahman.

Of It there is this teaching.—

That in the lightning which flashes forth, which makes one blink, and say "Ah!"—that "Ah!" refers to divinity.

Now with regard to oneself.—

That which comes, as it were, to the mind, by which one repeatedly remembers—that conception is Brahman![4]

(*Kena*, 3.1–12, 4.1–5)

9. *A Dying Father's Bequest of his Various Powers to His Son*

Now next, the Father-and-Son Ceremony, or the Transmission, as they call it.—

A father, when about to decease, summons his son. Having strewn the house with new grass, having built up the fire, having set down near it a vessel of water together with a dish, the father, wrapped around with a fresh garment, remains lying. The son, having come, lies down on top, touching organs with organs. Or he may, even, transmit to him seated face to face. Then he delivers over to him thus:—

Father: "My speech in you I would place!"

Son: "Your speech in me I take."

Father: "My breath in you I would place!"

Son: "Your breath in me I take."
Father: "My eye in you I would place!"
Son: "Your eye in me I take."
Father: "My ear in you I would place!"
Son: "Your ear in me I take."
Father: "My tastes in you I would place!"
Son: "Your tastes in me I would take!"
Father: "My deeds in you I would place!"
Son: "Your deeds in me I take."
Father: "My pleasure and pain in you I would place!"
Son: "Your pleasure and pain in me I take."
Father: "My bliss, delight, and procreation in you I would place!"
Son: "Your bliss, delight, and procreation in me I take."
Father: "My goings in you I would place!"
Son: "Your goings in me I take."
Father: "My mind in you I would place!"
Son: "Your mind in me I take."
Father: "My intelligence in you I would place!"
Son: "Your intelligence in me I take."

If, however, he should be unable to speak much, let the father say summarily: "My vital breaths in you I would place!" and the son reply: "Your vital breaths in me I take."

Then, turning to the right, he goes forth toward the east.

The father calls out after him: "May glory, sacred luster, and fame delight in you!"

Then the other looks over his left shoulder. Having hid his face with his hand, or having covered it with the edge of his garment, he says: "Heavenly worlds and desires do you obtain!"

If he should become well, the father should dwell under the lordship of his son, or he should wander around as a religious mendicant. If, however, he should decease, so let them furnish him as he ought to be furnished.[4]

(*Kauṣītaki*, 2.15)

10. *Naciketas and God Yama (Death)*

[A poor and pious Brahmana, Vājaśravasa, performs a sacrifice and gives as presents to the priests a few old and feeble cows. His son, Naciketas, feeling disturbed by the unreality of his father's observance of the sacrifice, proposes that he himself may be offered as offering to a priest. When he persisted in his request, his father in rage says, "Unto Yama, I give thee." Naciketas goes to the abode of Yama, and finding him absent, waits there for three days and nights unfed. Yama, on his return, offers three gifts in recompense for the delay and discomfort caused to Naciketas. For the first, Naciketas asked, "Let me return alive to my father." For the second, "Tell me how my good works may not be exhausted"; and for the third, "Tell me the way to conquer re-death."]

Naciketas and His Father

Desirous of the fruit of the sacrifice, Vājaśravasa, they say, gave away all that he possessed. He had a son by name Naciketas.

As the gifts were being taken to the priests, faith entered him, although but a mere boy; he thought.

Their water drunk, their grass eaten, their milk milked, their strength spent, joyless, verily, are those worlds, to which he, who presents such cows goes.

He said to his father, "O Sire, to whom wilt thou give me?" For a second and a third time he repeated, when the father said to him, "Unto Death shall I give thee."

Naciketas, "Of many sons or disciples I go as the first; of many, I go as the middling. What duty towards Yama that my father has to accomplish today, does he accomplish through me?

"Consider how it was with the forefathers; behold how it is with the later men; a mortal ripens like corn, and like corn is born again."

Naciketas in the House of Death

As a very fire a Brahmana guest enters into houses and the people do him this peace-offering; bring water, O Son of the Sun!

Hopes and expectation, friendship and joy, sacrifices and good works, sons, cattle and all are taken away from a person of little understanding in whose house a Brahmana remains unfed.

Yama's Address to Naciketas

"Since thou, a venerable guest, hast stayed in my house without food for three nights, I make obeisance to thee, O Brahmana. May it be well with me. Therefore, in return, choose thou three gifts."

Naciketas's First Wish

"That my father with allayed anxiety, with anger gone, may be gracious to me, O Death, and recognising me, greet me, when set free by you and this, I choose as the first gift of the three."

Yama said: "As of old through my favour will he sleep peacefully through nights, his anger gone, seeing thee released from the jaws of death."

Naciketas's Second Wish

Naciketas said: "In the world of heaven there is no fear whatever; thou are not there, nor does one fear old age. Crossing over both hunger and thirst, leaving sorrow behind, one rejoices in the world of heaven.

"Thou knowest, O Death, that fire sacrifice which is the aid to heaven. Describe it to me, full of faith, how the dwellers in heaven gain immortality. This I choose, as my second boon."

Yama said: "Knowing well as I do, that fire sacrifice which is the aid to heaven, I shall describe it to thee—learn it of me, O Naciketas. Know that fire to be the means of attaining the boundless world, as the support of the universe and as abiding in the secret place of the heart."

Yama described to him that the fire sacrifice which is the beginning of the world as also what kind of bricks are to be used in building the sacrificial altar, how many and in what manner. And Naciketas repeated all that just as it had been told: then, pleased with him, Death spoke again.

Yama, the great soul, extremely delighted, said to Naciketas: "I give thee here today another boon. By thine own name will this fire sacrifice become known. Take also this many-shaped chain.

"He who has lit the Naciketas fire thrice, associating with the three, performs the three acts, crosses over birth and death. Knowing the son of Brahma, the omniscient, resplendent and adorable and realising him, one obtains this everlasting peace.

"The wise man who has sacrificed thrice to Naciketas and who knows this three, and so knowing, performs meditation on fire throwing off first the bonds of death and overcoming sorrow, rejoices in the world of heaven.

"This is thy fire sacrifice, O Naciketas, which leading to heaven, which thou hast chosen for thy second boon. This first sacrifice people will call by thy name only. Choose now, O Naciketas, the third boon."

Naciketas's Third Wish

Naciketas said: "There is this doubt in regard to a man who has departed, some holding that he is and some that he is not. I would be instructed by thee in this knowledge. Of the boons, this is the third boon."

Yama said: "Even the gods of old had doubt on this point. It is not, indeed, easy to understand; so subtle in this truth. Choose another boon, O Naciketas. Do not press me. Release me from this."

Naciketas said: "Even the gods had doubt, indeed, as to this, and thou, O Death, sayest that it is not easy to understand. Instruct me for another teacher of it, like thee, is not to be got. No other boon is comparable to this at all."

Yama said: "Choose sons and grandsons that shall live a hundred years, cattle in plenty, elephants, gold and horses.

Choose vast expanses of land and life for thyself as many years as thou wilt.

"If thou deemest any boon like unto this, choose that as also wealth and long life. O Naciketas, prosper then on this vast earth. I will make thee the enjoyer of thy desires.

"Whatever desires are hard to attain in this world of mortals, ask for all those desires at thy will. Here are noble maidens with chariots and musical instruments: the like of them cannot be won by men. Be served by these whom I give to thee. O Naciketas, pray ask not about death."

Naciketas said: "Transient are these and they wear out, O Yama, the vigour of all the senses of men. All life, moreover, is brief. Thine be the chariots, thine the dance and song.

"Man is not to be contented with wealth. Shall we enjoy wealth when we have seen thee? Shall we live as long as thou are in power? That alone is still the boon chosen by me.

"Having approached the undecaying immortality, what decaying mortal on this earth below who now knows and meditates on the pleasures of beauty and love, will delight in an over-long life?

"Tell us that about which they doubt, O Death, what there is in the great passing-on. This boon which penetrates the mystery, no other than that does Naciketas choose."[5]

V. The *Gṛhya-sūtras*

Along with solemn ceremonies, there are "domestic" rites whose details are preserved in the "Domestic Aphorisms" of the Vedic period.

Except for certain adjustments, these practices have remained in general use in India. These collections are classified, like all Vedic texts, according to different "schools." They form part of the "unrevealed" portion of the Veda.

Marriage Ceremonies

Let him first examine the family of the intended bride or bridegroom.

Let him give the girl to a young man endowed with intelligence.

Let him marry a girl that shows the characteristics of intelligence, beauty, and moral conduct, and who is free from disease.

As the characteristics are difficult to discern, let him make eight lumps of earth, recite over the lumps the following formula, "Right has been born first, in the beginning: on the right truth is founded. For what destiny this girl is born, that may she attain here. What is true may that be seen," and let him say to the girl, "Take one of these."

If she chooses the lump taken from a field that yields two crops in one year, he may know, "Her offspring will be rich in food." If from a cow-stable, rich in cattle. If from the earth of an altar, rich in holy lustre. If from a pool which does not dry up, rich in everything. If from a gambling-place, addicted to gambling. If from a place where four roads meet, wandering to different directions. If from a barren spot, poor. If from a burial-ground, she will bring death to her husband. Having placed to the west of the fire a mill-stone, to the north-east a water-pot, he should sacrifice, while she takes hold of him. Standing, with his face turned to the west, he should with the formula, "I seize thy hand for the sake of happiness," seize her thumb if he desires that only male children may be born to him; her other fingers, if he is desirous of female children; the hand on the hair-side together with the thumb, if desirous of both.

Leading her three times round the fire and the water-pot, so that their right sides are turned towards the fire, he murmurs, "This am I, that are thou; that are thou, this am I; the heaven I, the earth thou. Come! Let us here marry. Let us beget offspring. Loving, bright, with genial mind may we live a hundred autumns."

Each time after he has lead her so round, he makes her tread on the stone with the words, "Tread on this stone; like a stone be firm. Overcome the enemies; tread the foes down."

Having first poured melted butter over her hands, her brother or a person acting in her brother's place pours fried grain twice over the wife's joined hands.

He pours again melted butter over what has been left of the sacrificed food, and over what has been cut off.

She should sacrifice the fried grain without opening her joined hands. Without that leading round the fire, she sacrifices grain with the neb of a basket towards herself.

He then loosens her two locks of hair, if they are made, i.e. if two tufts of wool are bound round her hair on the two sides.

He then causes her to step forward in a north-eastern direction seven steps with the words, "For sap with one step, for juice with two steps, for thriving five steps, for the seasons with six steps. Be friend with seven steps. So be thou devoted to me. Let us acquire many sons who may reach old age!"

Joining together their two heads, the bridegroom sprinkles them with water from the water-pot.

And she should dwell that night in the house of an old Brahmana woman whose husband is alive and whose children are alive.

When she sees the polar-star, the star Arundhatī, and the *ursa major*, let her break the silence and say, "May my husband live and I get offspring!"

If the newly-married couple have to make a journey to their new home, let him cause her to mount the chariot with the verse, "May Pūṣan lead thee from here holding thy hand!"

They constantly carry the nuptial fire in front.

At lovely places, trees, and cross-ways let him murmur the verse, "May no waylayers meet us!"

At every dwelling-place on their way let him look at the lookers on, with the verse, "Good luck brings this woman."

With the verse, "Here may delight fulfil itself to thee through offspring," he should make her enter the house.

Having given its place to the nuptial fire, and having spread to the west of it a bull's hide with the neck to the east, with the hair outside, he makes oblations, while she is sitting on that hide and takes hold of him; and he partakes of curds and gives thereof to her, or he besmears their two hearts with the rest of the butter of which he has sacrificed. From that time they should eat no saline food, they should be chaste, wear ornaments, sleep on the ground three nights or twelve nights; or one year, according to some teachers; thus, they say, a Seer will be born as their son.[6]

(*Asvalayana,* 1.5–8, with omissions)

VI. *The Dharma-Sūtras*

Though belonging to the Vedic canon, aphorisms relating to "*dharma*," that is to the Hindu norm, are the most ancient extant treatises of a juridical character which form part of *Smṛti.* They are, however, still concerned with religious preoccupations as can be seen in the exposition of the Brahmanical initiation which marked the admission of a young boy to the prerogatives of his social class. These texts must have appeared during the period between the sixth and the third centuries before our era.

1. *The Initiation*

The initiation is the consecration in accordance with the texts of the Veda, of a male who is desirous of and can make use of sacred knowledge.

Coming out of darkness, he indeed enters darkness, whom a man unlearned in the Vedas, initiates, and so does he who, without being learned in the Vedas, performs the rite of initiation.

As performer of this rite of initiation he shall seek to obtain a man in whose family sacred learning is hereditary, who himself possesses it, and who is devout in following the law.

And under him the sacred science must be studied until the end, provided the teacher does not fall off from the ordinances of the law.

He from whom the pupil gathers the knowledge of his religious duties is called the teacher.

Him he should never offend.

For he causes the pupil to be born a second time by imparting to him sacred learning.

The second birth is the best.

The father and the mother produce the body only.

Let him initiate a Brahmīn in spring, a Kṣatriya in summer, a Vaiśya in autumn, a Brahmīn in the eighth year after conception, a Kṣatriya in the eleventh year after conception, and a Vaiśya in the twelfth.

Now follows the enumeration of the years to be chosen for the fulfilment of some particular wish.

Let him initiate a person desirous of excellence in sacred learning in his seventh year, a person desirous of long life in his eighth year, a person desirous of manly vigour in his ninth year, a person desirous of food in his tenth year, a person desirous of strength in his eleventh year, a person desirous of cattle in his twelfth year.

There is no dereliction of duty, if the initiation takes place, in the case of a Brahmīn before the completion of the sixteenth year, in the case of a Kṣatriya before the completion of the twenty-second year, in the case of a Vaiśya before the completion of the twenty-fourth year. Let him be initiated at such an age that he may be able to perform the duties, which we shall declare below.

If the proper time for the initiation has passed, he shall observe for the space of two months the duties of a student, as observed by those who are studying the three Vedas.

After that he may be initiated, after that he shall bathe daily for one year, after that he may be instructed.

He, whose father and grandfather have not been initiated, and his two ancestors are called "slayers of the *brāhman.*"

Intercourse, eating, and intermarriage with them should be avoided.

If they wish it they may perform the following expiation: in the same manner as for the first neglect of the initiation, a penance of two months was prescribed, so they shall do penance for one year.

Afterwards they may be initiated, and then they must bathe daily.[7]

(*Āpastamba,* 1.1)

2. *Rules for an Ascetic*

Now the following vows are to be kept by an ascetic:

Abstention from injuring living beings, truthfulness, abstention from appropriating the property of others, continence, and liberality.

There are five minor vows, viz. abstention from anger, obedience towards the Guru, avoidance of rashness, cleanliness and purity in eating.

Now follows the rule for begging. Let him ask Brahmīns, both those who have houses and those who lead a wandering life, for alms, when the Vaiśvadeva offering has been finished.

Let him ask for it, prefacing his request with the word "*bhavat.*"

Let him stand begging no longer than the time required for milking a cow.

When he returns from begging, he lays the alms down in a pure place, washes his hands and feet, and announces what he obtained to the sun.

Giving, compassionately, portions of his food to the living beings, and sprinkling the remainder with water, he shall eat it as if it were a medicine.

Let him eat food, given without asking, regarding which nothing has been settled beforehand and which has reached him accidentally, so much only as is sufficient to sustain life.

Now they quote also the following verses: "Eight mouthfuls

make the meal of an ascetic, sixteen that of a hermit in the woods, thirty-two that of a householder, an unlimited quantity that of a student.

"Alms may either be obtained from men of the three castes, or the food given by a single brāhmaṇa may be eaten; or he may obtain food from men of all castes, and not eat that given by a single Brahmīn."

Now they quote the following special rules for the case that the teachers explain the doctrine of the Upaniṣads: "Diligently standing in the day-time, keeping silence, sitting at night with crossed legs, bathing three times a day, and eating at the fourth, sixth, or eighth meal-time only, he shall subsist entirely on rice grains, oil-cake, food prepared from barley, sour milk, and milk."

It is declared in the Veda, "On that occasion he shall rigidly keep silence; pressing the teeth together he may converse, without opening his mouth, as much as is necessary with teachers deeply versed in the three Vedas and with ascetics possessing a great knowledge of the scriptures, not with women, not when he would break his vow."

Let him keep only one of the rules which enjoin standing in the day-time, rigid silence, and sitting at night with crossed legs; let him not keep all three together.

It is declared in the Veda, "And he who has gone there may eat, in times of distress, a small quantity of the food prescribed by his vow after having partaken of other dishes, provided he does not break his vow.

"Eight things do not cause him who is intent on standing in the day-time, keeping rigid silence, sitting at night with crossed legs, bathing three times a day, and eating at the fourth, sixth, or eighth meal-time only, to break his vow, viz. water, roots, clarified butter, milk, sacrificial food, the wish of a Brahmīn, an order of his teacher, and medicine.

"An ascetic shall keep no fire, have no house, no home, and no protector. He may enter a village in order to collect alms, and emit speech at the private recitation of the Veda."[7]

(*Baudhāyana,* 2.10, 18)

3. *General Rules*

Now, therefore, the desire to know the sacred law for their welfare should arise in initiated men.

He who knows and follows the sacred law is called a righteous man.

He becomes most worthy of praise in this world and after death gains heaven.

The sacred law has been settled by the revealed texts and by the tradition of the sages.

On failure of rules given in these two sources the practice of the Śiṣṭas[a] has authority.

But he whose heart is free from desire is called a Śiṣṭa.

Acts sanctioned by the sacred law are those for which no worldly cause is perceptible.

The country of the Āryas[b] lies to the east of the region where the river Sarasvatī disappears, to the west of the Black-forest, to the north of the Pāripātra mountains, to the south of the Himālaya.

Acts productive of spiritual merit, and customs which are approved of in that country, must be everywhere acknowledged as authoritative.

But not different ones, i.e. those of countries where laws opposed to those of Āryāvarta[c] prevail.

Some declare the country of the Āryas to be situated between the rivers Gaṅgā and Yamunā.

Others state as an alternative, that spiritual pre-eminence is found as far as the black-antelope grazes.

Manu has declared that the peculiar laws of countries, castes, and families may be followed in the absence of rules of the revealed texts.

Sinful men are, he who sleeps at sunrise or at sunset, he who has deformed nails or black teeth, he whose younger brother was married first, he who married before his elder brother, the husband of an elder sister whose younger sister was married first, he who extinguishes the sacred fires, and he who forgets the Veda through neglect of the daily recitation.

They state that there are five mortal sins.

Viz. violating a Guru's bed, drinking (the spirituous liquor called) *surā*, slaying a learned Brahmīn, stealing the gold of a Brahmīn, and associating with outcastes, either by entering into spiritual or matrimonial connexion with them.

Now they quote also the following verse: "He who during a year associates with an outcaste becomes likewise an outcaste; not by sacrificing for him, by teaching him or by forming a matrimonial alliance with him, but by using the same carriage or seat."

A minor offence causing loss of caste, is committed by him who after beginning an Agnihotra sacrifice forsakes the sacred fires, and by him who offends a Guru, by an atheist, by him who takes his livelihood from atheists, and by him who sells the Soma plant.

Three wives are permitted to a Brahmīn according to the order of the castes, two to a Kṣatriya, one to a Vaiśya and to a Śūdra.

Some declare that twice-born men may marry even a female of the Śūdra caste, like those other wives, without the recitation of Vedic texts.

Let him not act thus.

For in consequence of such a marriage the degradation of the family certainly ensues, and after death the loss of heaven.

There are six marriage-rites,

Viz. that of Brahmā, that of the gods, that of the Ṛṣis, that of the Gāndharvas, that of the Kṣatriyas, and that of men.[d]

If the father, pouring out a libation of water, gives his daughter to a suitor, that is called the Brahmā-rite.

If the father gives his daughter, decking her with ornaments, to an officiating priest, whilst a sacrifice is being performed, that is called the Daiva-rite.

And if the father gives his daughter for a cow and a bull, that is called the Ārṣa-rite.

If a lover takes a loving female of equal caste, that is called the Gāndharva-rite.

If they forcibly abduct a damsel, destroying her relatives by strength of arms, that is called the Kṣātra-rite.

If, after making a bargain with the father, a suitor marries a damsel purchased for money, that is called the Mānuṣa-rite.

The purchase of a wife is mentioned in the following passage of the Veda, "Therefore one hundred cows besides a chariot should be given to the father of the bride."

The three lower castes shall live according to the teaching of the Brahmīns.

The Brahmīns shall declare their duties,

And the king shall govern them accordingly.

But a king who rules in accordance with the sacred law, may take the sixth part of the wealth of his subjects,

Except from Brahmīns.

It has been declared in the Veda, "But he obtains the sixth part of the merit which Brahmīns gain by sacrifices and charitable works."

It is further stated in the Veda, "The Brahmīn makes the Veda rich; the Brahmīn saves from misfortune; therefore the Brahmīn shall not be made a source of subsistence. Soma is his king."

Further another passage says, "After death bliss awaits the king who does not oppress Brahmīns."[7]

(*Vasiṣṭha,* 1.1–46)

[a] The cultivated men.
[b] Northern and central India.
[c] The sacred land inhabitated by the Āryas.
[d] These are the six kinds of marriage, defined in the next paragraphs.

4. *The Duties of a King*

The king is master of all, with the exception of Brahmīns.

He shall be holy in acts and speech,

Fully instructed in the threefold sacred science and in logic,

Pure, of subdued senses, surrounded by companions possessing excellent qualities and by the means for upholding his rule.

He shall be impartial towards his subjects;

And he shall do what is good for them.

All, excepting Brahmīns, shall worship him who is seated on a higher seat, while they themselves sit on a lower one.

The Brahmīns, also, shall honour him.

He shall protect the castes and orders in accordance with justice;

And those who leave the path of duty, he shall lead back to it.

For it is declared in the Veda that he obtains a share of the spiritual merit gained by his subjects.

And he shall select as his domestic priest a Brahmīn who is learned in the Vedas, of noble family, eloquent, handsome, of a suitable age, and of a virtuous disposition, who lives righteously and who is austere.

With his assistance he shall fulfil his religious duties.

For it is declared in the Veda: "Kṣatriyas, who are assisted by Brahmīns, prosper and do not fall into distress."

He shall, also, take heed of that which astrologers and interpreters of omens tell him.

For some declare, that the acquisition of wealth and security depend also upon that.

He shall perform in the fire of the hall the rites ensuring prosperity which are connected with expiations, festivals, a prosperous march, long life, and auspiciousness; as well as those that are intended to cause enmity, to subdue enemies, to destroy them by incantations, and to cause their misfortune.

Officiating priests shall perform the other sacrifices according to the precepts of the Veda.

His administration of justice shall be regulated by the Veda, the Institutes of the Sacred Law, the Aṅgas,[a] and the Purāṇa.[b]

The laws of countries, castes, and families, which are not opposed to the sacred records, have also authority.

Cultivators, traders, herdsmen, money-lenders, and artisans have authority to lay down rules for their respective classes.

Having learned the state of affairs from those who in each class have authority to speak, he shall give the legal decision.

Reasoning is a means for arriving at the truth.

Coming to a conclusion through that, he shall decide properly.

If the evidence is conflicting, he shall learn the truth from Brahmīns who are well versed in the threefold sacred lore,[c] and give his decision accordingly.

For, if he acts thus, blessings will attend him in this world and the next.[7]

(*Gautama,* 11.1–26)

[a] The six ancillary "members" of the Veda.
[b] The book of "Antiquities."
[c] The three Vedas.

VII. The *Manu-Smṛti*

The *Mānava-dharma-śāstra* or *Laws of Manu* constitute a classic of Indian juridical theory. This work, which may perhaps be dated one or two centuries before our era, condenses in the form of diversified maxims all of the content of *dharma,* whether it be the specifically religious rules, institutions, customs and ethical precepts which dominate an individual's existence; whether it be the individual established in the world (and, consequently, subjected to the directions of social castes and of *āśramas*) or the individual isolated from the world (ascetic). These rules are presented within the framework of a large cosmogonic fresco, a large part of which is cited below (No. 7): Manu is here the primordial man who receives the revelation of the supreme designs of

Brahman and is at the same time the promulgator of *Smṛti* or "Memorized tradition" (secondarily issued from the *Śruti* or "Direct Revelation").

No. 8 and No. 9 are taken from later texts of *Smṛti* (which are equally of an indefinite date), the *Viṣṇu Smṛti,* and the *Nārada Smṛti.*

1. *On Transmigration*

Action, which springs from the mind, from speech, and from the body, produces either good or evil results; by action are caused the various conditions of men, the highest, the middling, and the lowest.

Know that the mind is the instigator here below, even to that action which is connected with the body, and which is of three kinds, has three locations, and falls under ten heads.

Coveting the property of others, thinking in one's heart of what is undesirable, and adherence to false doctrines are the three kinds of sinful mental action.

Abusing others, speaking untruth, detracting from the merits of all men, and talking idly shall be the four kinds of evil verbal action.

Taking what has not been given, injuring creatures without the sanction of the law, and holding criminal intercourse with another man's wife are declared to be the three kinds of wicked bodily action.

A man obtains the result of a good or evil mental act in his mind, that of a verbal act in his speech, that of a bodily act in his body.

In consequence of many sinful acts committed with his body, a man becomes in the next birth something inanimate, in consequence of sins committed by speech, a bird, or a beast, and in consequence of mental sins he is re-born in a low caste.[8]

(12.3–9, 11)

2. *Rules for a Householder*

Having dwelt with a teacher during the fourth part of a man's life, a Brahmīn shall live during the second quarter of his existence in his house, after he has wedded a wife.

A Brahmīn must seek a means of subsistence which either causes no, or at least little pain to others, and live by that except in times of distress.

For the purpose of gaining bare subsistence, let him accumulate property by following those irreproachable occupations which are prescribed for his caste, without unduly fatiguing his body.

Let him never, for the sake of subsistence, follow the ways of the world; let him live the pure, straightforward, honest life of a Brahmīn.

He who desires happiness must strive after a perfectly contented disposition and control himself; for happiness has contentment for its root, the root of unhappiness is the contrary disposition.

Whether he be rich or even in distress, let him not seek wealth through pursuits to which men cleave, nor by forbidden occupations, nor let him accept presents from any giver whosoever he may be.

Let him not, out of desire for enjoyments, attach himself to any sensual pleasures, and let him carefully obviate an excessive attachment to them, by reflecting on their worthlessness in his heart.

Let him avoid all means of acquiring wealth which impede the study of the Veda; let him maintain himself anyhow, but study, because that devotion to the Veda-study secures the realisation of his aims.

Let him walk here on earth, bringing his dress, speech, and thoughts to a conformity with his age, his occupation, his wealth, his sacred learning, and his race.[8]

(4.1–3, 11–12, 15–18)

3. *Rules for the Ascetic*

Having passed the third part of a man's natural term of life in the forest, he may live as an ascetic during the fourth part of his existence, after abandoning all attachment to worldly objects.

He who after passing from order to order, after offering sacrifices and subduing his senses, becomes, tired with giving alms and offerings of food, an ascetic, gains bliss after death.

When he has paid the three debts, let him apply his mind to the attainment of final liberation; he who seeks it without having paid his debts sinks downwards.

Having studied the Vedas in accordance with the rule, having begat sons according to the sacred law, and having offered sacrifices according to his ability, he may direct his mind to the attainment of final liberation.

Departing from his house fully provided with the means of purification, let him wander about absolutely silent, and caring nothing for enjoyments that may be offered to him.

He shall neither possess a fire, nor a dwelling; he may go to a village for his food; he shall be indifferent to everything, firm of purpose, meditating and concentrating his mind on *brāhman*.

Let him not desire to die, let him not desire to live; let him wait for his appointed time, as a servant waits for the payment of his wages.

Let him put down his foot purified by his sight, let him drink water purified by straining with a cloth, let him utter speech purified by truth, let him keep his heart pure.

Delighting in what refers to the Soul, sitting in the postures prescribed by the Yoga, independent of external help, entirely abstaining from sensual enjoyments, with himself for his only companion, he shall live in this world, desiring the bliss of final liberation.

Let him reflect on the transmigrations of men, caused by their sinful deeds, on their falling into hell, and on the torments in the world of Yama,[a] on the separation from their dear ones, on their union with hated men, on their being overpowered by age and being tormented with diseases, on the departure of the individual soul from this body and its new birth in another womb, and on its wanderings through ten thousand millions of existences, on the infliction of pain on embodied spirits, which is caused by demerit, and the gain of eternal bliss, which is caused by the attainment of their highest aim, gained through spiritual merit.[8]

(6.33 ff., *passim*)

[a] Hell.

4. *Duties of Women*

By a girl, by a young woman, or even by an aged one, nothing must be done independently, even in her own house.

In childhood a female must be subject to her father, in youth to her husband; when her lord is dead, to her sons; a woman must never be independent.

She must not seek to separate herself from her father, husband, or sons; by leaving them she would make both her own and her husband's families contemptible.

She must always be cheerful, clever in the management of her household affairs, careful her utensils, and economical in expenditure.

Him to whom her father may give her, or her brother with the father's permission, she shall obey as long as he lives, and when he is dead, she must not insult his memory.

For the sake of procuring good fortune to brides, the recitation of benedictory texts, and the sacrifice to the Lord of creatures are used at weddings; but the betrothal by the father or guardian is the cause of the husband's dominion over his wife.

The husband who wedded her with sacred texts, always gives happiness to his wife, both in season and out of season, in this world and in the next.

Though destitute of virtue, or seeking pleasure elsewhere, or devoid of good qualities, yet a husband must be constantly worshipped as a god by a faithful wife.

No sacrifice, no vow, no fast must be performed by women apart from their husbands; if a wife obeys her husband, she will for that reason alone be exalted in heaven.

A faithful wife, who desires to dwell after death with her husband, must never do anything that might displease him who took her hand, whether he be alive or dead.

At her pleasure let her emaciate her body by living on pure flowers, roots, and fruit; but she must never mention the name of another man after her husband has died.

Until death let her be patient of hardships, self-controlled, and chaste, and strive to fulfil that most excellent duty which is prescribed for wives who have one husband only.

By violating her duty towards her husband, a wife is disgraced in this world; after death she enters the womb of a jackal, and is tormented by diseases, the punishment of her sin.

She who, controlling her thoughts, words, and deeds, never slights her lord, resides after death with her husband in heaven, and is called a virtuous wife.

A twice-born man, versed in the sacred law, shall burn a wife of equal caste who conducts herself thus and dies before him, with the sacred fires used for the Agnihotra, and with the sacrificial implements.

Having thus, at the funeral, given the sacred fires to his wife who dies before him, he may marry again, and again kindle the fires.[8]

(*Ibid.*, 5.147–158, 164, 165, 167, 168)

5. *King and Punishment*

Punishment alone governs all created beings, punishment alone protects them, punishment watches over them while they sleep; the wise declare punishment to be the law.

If punishment is properly inflicted after due consideration, it makes all people happy; but inflicted without consideration, it destroys everything.

If the king did not, without tiring, inflict punishment on

those worthy to be punished, the stronger would roast the weaker, like fish on a spit;

The crow would eat the sacrificial cake and the dog would lick the sacrificial viands, and ownership would not remain with any one, the lower ones would usurp the place of the higher ones.

The whole world is kept in order by punishment, for a guiltless man is hard to find; through fear of punishment the whole world yields the enjoyments which it owes.

The gods, the Dānavas, the Gāndharvas, the Rākṣasas,[a] the bird and snake deities even give the enjoyments due from them only, if they are tormented by the fear of punishment.

All castes would be corrupted by intermixture, all barriers would be broken through, and all men would rage against each other in consequence of mistakes with respect to punishment.

But where Punishment with a black hue and red eyes stalks about, destroying sinners, there the subjects are not disturbed, provided that he who inflicts it discerns well.[8]

(7.18, 20–25)

[a] Classes of demons or demigods.

6. *The Spiritual Merit*

Giving no pain to any creature, let him slowly accumulate spiritual merit, for the sake of acquiring a companion to the next world, just as the white ant gradually raises its hill.

For in the next world neither father, nor mother, nor wife, nor sons, nor relations stay to be his companions; spiritual merit alone remains with him.

Single is each being born; single it dies; single it enjoys the reward of its virtue; single it suffers the punishment of its sin.

Leaving the dead body on the ground like a log of wood, or a clod of earth, the relatives depart with averted faces; but spiritual merit follows the soul.

Let him therefore always slowly accumulate spiritual merit,

in order that it may be his companion after death; for without merit as his companion he will traverse a gloom difficult to traverse.

That companion speedily conducts the man who is devoted to duty and effaces his sins by austerities, to the next world, radiant and clothed with an ethereal body.[8]

(4.238–243)

7. *The Creation of the World*

This universe existed in the shape of Darkness, unperceived, destitute of distinctive marks, unattainable by reasoning, unknowable, wholly immersed, as it were, in deep sleep.

Then the divine Self-existent, himself indiscernible, but making all this, the great Elements and the rest, discernible, appeared with irresistible creative power, dispelling the darkness.

He who can be perceived by the internal organ alone, who is subtile, indiscernible, and eternal, who contains all created beings and is inconceivable, shone forth of his own will.

He, desiring to produce beings of many kinds from his own body, first with a thought created the waters, and placed his seed in them.

That seed became a golden egg, in brilliancy equal to the sun; in that egg he himself was born as Brahman, the progenitor of the whole world.

From that first cause, which is indiscernible, eternal, and both real and unreal, was produced that male, who is famed in this world under the appellation of Brahman.

The divine one resided in that egg during a whole year, then he himself by his thought alone divided it into two halves;

And out of those two halves he formed heaven and earth, between them the middle sphere, the eight points of the horizon, and the eternal abode of the waters.

But in the beginning he assigned their several names, actions, and conditions to all created beings, even according to the words of the Veda.

To whatever course of action the Lord at first appointed each kind of beings, that alone it had spontaneously adopted in each succeeding creation.

Whatever he assigned to each at the first creation, noxiousness or harmlessness, gentleness or ferocity, virtue or sin, truth or falsehood, that clung afterwards spontaneously to it.

As at the change of the seasons each season of its own accord assumes its distinctive marks, even so corporeal beings resume in new births their appointed course of action.

The various conditions in this always terrible and constantly changing circle of births and deaths to which created beings are subject, are stated to begin with that of Brahman, and to end with that of the immovable creatures.

When he whose power is incomprehensible had thus produced the universe, he disappeared in himself, repeatedly suppressing one period by means of the other.

When that divine one wakes, then this world stirs; when he slumbers tranquilly, then the universe sinks to sleep.

But when he reposes in calm sleep, the corporeal beings whose nature is action, desist from their actions and mind becomes inert.

When they are absorbed all at once in that great soul, then he who is the soul of all beings sweetly slumbers, free from all care and occupation.

When this soul has entered darkness, it remains for a long time united with the organs of sensation, but performs not its functions; it then leaves the corporeal frame.

Thus he, the imperishable one, by alternately waking and slumbering, incessantly revivifies and destroys this whole movable and immovable creation.

But hear now the brief description of the duration of a night and a day of Brahman and of the several ages of the world according to their order.

They declare that the Kṛta[a] age consists of four thousand years of the gods; the twilight preceding it consists of as many hundreds, and the twilight following it of the same number.

In the other three ages[b] with their twilights preceding and following, the thousands and hundreds are diminished by one in each.

These twelve thousand years which thus have been just mentioned as the total of four human ages, are called one age of the gods.

But know that the sum of one thousand ages of the gods makes one day of Brahman, and that his night has the same length.

Those only, who know that the holy day of Brahman, indeed, ends after the completion of one thousand ages of the gods and that his night lasts as long, are really men acquainted with the length of days and nights.

At the end of that day and night he who was asleep, awakes and, after awaking, creates mind, which is both real and unreal.

Mind, impelled by Brahman's desire to create, performs the work of creation by modifying itself, thence ether is produced; they declare that sound is the quality of the latter.

But from ether, modifying itself, springs the pure, powerful wind, the vehicle of all perfumes; that is held to possess the quality of touch.

Next from wind, modifying itself, proceeds the brilliant light, which illuminates and dispels darkness; that is declared to possess the quality of colour;

And from light, modifying itself, is produced water, possessing the quality of taste, from water earth which has the quality of smell; such is the creation in the beginning.

The before-mentioned age of the gods, or twelve thousand of their years, being multiplied by seventy-one, constitutes what is here named the Period of a Manu.

The Periods of a Manu, the creations and destructions of the world, are numberless; sporting, as it were, Brahma repeats this again and again.

In the Kṛta age, Dharma[c] is four-footed and entire, and so is Truth; nor does any gain accrue to men by uprighteousness.

In the other three ages, by reason of unjust gains, Dharma is deprived successively of one foot, and through the prevalence of theft, falsehood, and fraud the merit gained by men is diminished by one fourth in each.

Men are free from disease, accomplish all their aims, and live four hundred years in the Kṛta age, but in the Tretā and in each of the succeeding ages their life is lessened by one quarter.

The life of mortals, mentioned in the Veda, the desired results of sacrificial rites and the supernatural power of embodied spirits are fruits proportioned among men according to the character of the age.

One set of duties is prescribed for men in the Kṛta age, different ones in the Tretā and in the Dvāpara, and again another set in the Kali, in proportion as those ages decrease in length.

In the Kṛta age the chief virtue is declared to be the performance of austerities, in the Tretā divine knowledge, in the Dvāpara the performance of sacrifices, in the Kali liberality alone.

But in order to protect this universe He, the most resplendent one, assigned separate duties and occupations to those who sprang from his mouth, arms, thighs, and feet.

To Brahmīns he assigned teaching and studying the Veda, sacrificing for their own benefit and for others, giving and accepting of alms.

The Kṣatriya he commanded to protect the people, to bestow gifts, to offer sacrifices, to study the Veda, and to abstain from attaching himself to sensual pleasures;

The Vaiśya to tend cattle, to bestow gifts, to offer sacrifices, to study the Veda, to trade, to lend money, and to cultivate land.

One occupation only the lord prescribed to the Śūdra, to serve meekly even these other three castes.

In this work the sacred law has been fully stated as well as the good and bad qualities of human actions and the immemorial rule of conduct, to be followed by all the four castes.

The rule of conduct is transcendent law, whether it be

taught in the revealed texts or in the sacred tradition; hence a twice-born man who possesses regard for himself, should be always careful to follow it.

The creation of the universe, the rule of the sacraments, the ordinances of studentship, and the respectful behaviour towards *Gurus,*[d] the most excellent rule of bathing on return from the teacher's house,

The law of marriage and the description of the various marriage-rites, the regulations for the great sacrifices and the eternal rule of the funeral sacrifices,

The description of the modes of gaining subsistence and the duties of a snataka,[e] the rules regarding lawful and forbidden food, the purification of men and of things,

The laws concerning women, the law of hermits, the manner of gaining final emancipation and of renouncing the world, the whole duty of a king and the manner of deciding lawsuits,

The rules for the examination of witnesses, the laws concerning husband and wife, the law of inheritance and division, the law concerning gambling and the removal of men nocuous like thorns,

The law concerning the behaviour of Vaiśyas and Śūdras, the origin of the mixed castes, the law for all castes in times of distress and the law of penances,

The threefold course of transmigrations, the result of good or bad actions, the manner of attaining supreme bliss and the examination of the good and bad qualities of actions,

The primeval laws of countries, castes, of families, and the rules concerning heretics and companies of traders and the like—all that Manu has declared in these Institutes.[8]

(1.5–118, with several omissions)

[a] The first or golden age.

[b] The Tretā, Dvāpara, and Kali age, the last being the present age—and worst of all.

[c] The sacred law.

[d] Spiritual teachers.

[e] A Brahmin who has completed his training.

8. *Death and Human Action*

Even were he to die with him, a kinsman is unable to follow his dead relative: all excepting his wife are forbidden to follow him on the path of Yama.[a]

Virtue alone will follow him, wherever he may go; therefore do your duty unflinchingly in this wretched world.

To-morrow's business should be done to-day, and the afternoon's business in the forenoon; for death will not wait, whether a person has done it or not.

While his mind is fixed upon his field, or traffic, or his house, or while his thoughts are engrossed by some other beloved object, death suddenly carries him away as his prey, as a she-wolf catches a lamb.

Time is no one's friend and no one's enemy: when the effect of his acts in a former existence, by which his present existence is caused, has expired, he snatches a man away forcibly.

He will not die before his time has come, even though he has been pierced by a thousand shafts; he will not live after his time is out, even though he has only been touched by the point of a blade of Kuśa grass.

Neither drugs, nor magical formulas, nor burnt-offerings, nor prayers will save a man who is in the bonds of death or old age.

An impending evil cannot be averted even by a hundred precautions; what reason then for you to complain?

Even as a calf finds his mother among a thousand cows, an act formerly done is sure to find the perpetrator.

Of existing beings the beginnings is unknown, the middle of their career is known, and the end again unknown; what reason then for you to complain?

As the body of mortals undergoes the vicissitudes of infancy, youth, and old age, even so will it be transformed into another body hereafter; a sensible man is not mistaken about that.

As a man puts on new clothes in this world, throwing aside

those which he formerly wore, even so the self of man puts on new bodies, which are in accordance with his acts in a former life.

No weapons will hurt the self of man, no fire burn it, no waters moisten it, and no wind dry it up.

It is not to be hurt, not to be burnt, not to be moistened, and not to be dried up; it is imperishable, perpetual, unchanging, immovable, without beginning.

It is further said to be immaterial, passing all thought, and immutable. Knowing the self of man to be such, you must not grieve for the destruction of his body.[9]

(*Viṣṇu-smṛti,* 20.39–53)

[a] The god of death.

9. *The Power of Truth*

Truth is said to be the one unequalled means of purification of the soul. Truth is the ladder by which man ascends to heaven, as a ferry plies from one bank of a river to the other.

If truth and a thousand horse-sacrifices are balanced against one another, it will be found that truth weighs more heavily than a thousand horse-sacrifices.

A tank is better than a hundred wells, an offering better than a hundred tanks, a son better than a hundred offerings, and truth better than a hundred sons.

It is truth which makes the earth bear all beings, truth which makes the sun rise.

It is through truth that winds blow, and that the waters flow.

Truth is the greatest gift, truth is the most efficacious kind of austerity, truth is the highest duty in the world, thus it has been revealed to us.

The gods are truth simply, the human race is falsehood. He whose mind is persistent in truth, obtains a divine state in this world even.

Speak truth and discard falsehood. It is through truth that

thou shalt attain heaven. By uttering a falsehood thou wilt precipitate thyself into a most dreadful hellish abode.

And in the hells the merciless attendants of Yama,[a] endowed with great strength, will cut off thy tongue and strike thee with swords, constantly,

And attack and pierce thee with spears, while thou art wailing helpless. When thou art standing, they will fell thee to the ground and fling thee into the flames.

After having sustained thus for a long while the acute tortures of hell, thou shalt enter in this world the horrid bodies of vultures, crows, and other despicable creatures.

Having discovered these evils with which falsehood is attended, and knowing, on the other hand, the advantages resulting from veracity, thou must speak truth and thereby save thyself. Do not ruin thyself wantonly.[10]

(*Nārada-smṛti,* 1.210–220)

[a] The god of death.

VIII. The *Bhagavad-gītā*

At the time when the warrior Arjuna is about to engage in final battle against his enemies, the Kauravas, he is seized with fear at the possibility of having to shed blood. He questions his chariot companion, Kṛṣṇa. The latter removes his hesitation: Arjuna must perform his duty as a warrior; besides, Kṛṣṇa tells him, life and death are of little worth when compared with eternal values. That is how the famous poem, *The Celestial Song*, begins.

Gradually revealing himself to Arjuna as the Supreme Lord, Kṛṣṇa teaches action without desire, which conducts a human being to Liberation.

This poem was perhaps attached to the Epic, the

Mahā-Bhārata; it is of an indefinite date, perhaps contemporaneous with the beginning of our era. The *Bhagavad-gītā* has rightly been called the Gospel of Kṛṣṇaism.

1. *The Wise Facing Death*

Kṛṣṇa's Rebuke and Exhortation to Be Brave

The recitant said:

To Arjuna, who was thus overcome by pity, whose eyes were filled with tears and troubled and who was much depressed in mind, Kṛṣṇa spoke this word.

The Blessed Lord said:

Whence has come to thee this dejection of spirit in this hour of crisis? It is unknown to men of noble mind; it does not lead to heaven; on earth it causes disgrace, O Arjuna.

Yield not to this unmanliness, O Arjuna, for it does not become thee. Cast off this petty faintheartedness and arise, O Oppressor of the foes.

Arjuna's Doubts Are Unresolved

Arjuna said:

How shall I strike Bhīsma and Droṇa who are worthy of worship, O Kṛṣṇa, with arrows in battle, O Slayer of foes?

It is better to live in this world by begging than to slay these honoured teachers. Though they are mindful of their gains, they are my teachers and by slaying them, only, I would enjoy in this world delights which are smeared with blood.

Nor do we know which for us is better, whether we conquer them or they conquer us. The sons of Dhṛtarāṣṭra, whom if we slew we should not care to live, are standing before us in battle array.

My very being is stricken with the weakness of pity. With my mind bewildered about my duty, I ask Thee. Tell me, for certain, which is better. I am Thy pupil; teach me, who am seeking refuge in Thee.

I do not see what will drive away this sorrow which dries

up my senses even if I should attain rich and unrivalled kingdom on earth or even the sovereignty of the gods.

The recitant said:

Having thus addressed Kṛṣṇa, the mighty Arjuna said to Kṛṣṇa: "I will not fight" and became silent.

To him thus depressed in the midst of the two armies, O Bhārata, Kṛṣṇa, smiling as it were, spoke this word.

We Should Not Grieve for What Is Imperishable

The Blessed Lord said:

Thou grievest for those whom thou shouldst not grieve for, and yet thou speakest words about wisdom. Wise men do not grieve for the dead or for the living.

Never was there a time when I was not, nor thou, nor these lords of men, nor will there ever be a time hereafter when we shall cease to be.

As the soul passes in this body through childhood, youth and age, even so is its taking on of another body. The sage is not perplexed by this.

Contacts with their objects, O Son of Kuntī, give rise to cold and heat, pleasure and pain.

They come and go and do not last for ever, these learn to endure, O Arjuna.

The man who is not troubled by these, O Chief of men, who remains the same in pain and pleasure, who is wise makes himself fit for eternal life.

Of the non-existent there is no coming to be; of the existent there is no ceasing to be.

The conclusion about these two has been perceived by the seers of truth.

Know thou that that by which all this is pervaded is indestructible. Of this immutable being, no one can bring about the destruction.

It is said that these bodies of the eternal soul which is indestructible and incomprehensible come to an end. Therefore fight, O Arjuna.

He who thinks that this slays and he who thinks that this is slain; both of them fail to perceive the truth; this one neither slays nor is slain.

He is never born, nor does he die at any time, nor having once come to be does he again cease to be. He is unborn, eternal, permanent and primeval. He is not slain when the body is slain.

He who knows that it is indestructible and eternal, uncreate and unchanging, how can such a person slay any one, O Arjuna, or cause any one to slay?

Just as a person casts off worn-out garments and puts on others that are new, even so does the soul cast off worn-out bodies and take on others that are new.

Weapons do not cleave this self, fire does not burn him; waters do not make him wet; nor does the wind make him dry.

He is uncleavable, He cannot be burnt. He can be neither wetted nor dried. He is eternal, all-pervading, unchanging and immovable. He is the same for ever.

He is said to be unmanifest, unthinkable and unchanging. Therefore, knowing him as such, thou shouldst not grieve.

We Should Not Grieve over What Is Perishable

Even if thou thinkest that the self is perpetually born and perpetually dies, even then, O Mighty-armed, thou shouldst not grieve.

For to the one that is born death is certain and certain is birth for the one that has died. Therefore for what is unavoidable, thou shouldst not grieve.

Beings are unmanifest in their beginnings, manifest in the middle and unmanifest again in their ends. O Arjuna, what is there in this for lamentation?

One looks upon Him as a marvel, another likewise speaks of Him as a marvel: another hears of Him as a marvel; and even after hearing, no one whatsoever has known Him.

The dweller in the body of every one, O Arjuna, is eternal and can never be slain, therefore thou shouldst not grieve for any creature.

The Characteristics of the Perfect Sage

Arjuna said:

What is the description of the man who has this firmly founded wisdom, whose being is steadfast in spirit, O Kṛṣṇa? How does the man of settled intelligence speak, how does he sit, how does he walk?

The Blessed Lord said:

When a man puts away all the desires of his mind, O Arjuna, and when his spirit is content in itself, then is he called stable in intelligence.

He whose mind is untroubled in the midst of sorrows and is free from eager desire amid pleasures, he from whom passion, fear, and rage have passed away, he is called a sage of settled intelligence.

He who is without affection on any side, who does not rejoice or loathe as he obtains good or evil, his intelligence is firmly set in wisdom.

He who draws away the senses from the objects of sense on every side as a tortoise draws in his limbs into the shell, his intelligence is firmly set in wisdom.

The objects of sense turn away from the embodied soul who abstains from feeding on them but the taste for them remains. Even the taste turns away when the Supreme is seen.

Even though a man may ever strive for perfection and be ever so discerning, O Son of Kuntī, his impetuous senses will carry off his mind by force.

Having brought all the senses under control, he should remain firm in *Yoga* intent on Me; for he, whose senses are under control, his intelligence is firmly set.

When a man dwells in his mind on the objects of sense, attachment to them is produced.

From attachment springs desire and from desire comes anger.

From anger arises bewilderment, from bewilderment loss of memory; and from loss of memory the destruction of intelligence and from the destruction of intelligence he perishes.

But a man of disciplined mind, who moves among the

objects of sense, with the senses under control and free from attachment and aversion, attains purity of spirit.

And in that purity of spirit, there is produced for him an end of all sorrow; the intelligence of such a man of pure spirit is soon established in the peace of the self.

For the uncontrolled, there is no intelligence; nor for the uncontrolled is there the power of concentration and for him without concentration, there is no peace and for the unpeaceful, how can there be happiness?

When the mind runs after the roving senses, it carries away the understanding, even as a wind carries away a ship on the waters.

Therefore, O Mighty-armed, he whose senses are all withdrawn from their objects—his intelligence is firmly set.

What is night for all beings is the time of waking for the disciplined soul; and what is the time of waking for all beings is night for the sage who sees.

He unto whom all desires enter as waters into the sea, which, though ever being filled in ever motionless, attains to peace and not he who hugs his desires.

He who abandons all desires and acts free from longing, without any sense of mineness or egotism, he attains to peace.

This is the divine state, O Arjuna, having attained thereto, one is not again bewildered; fixed in that state at the hour of death one can attain to the bliss of God.[11]

(2.1–30, 54–72)

2. *Kṛṣṇa Manifests Himself in His glory*

Of many mouths and eyes,
Of many wondrous aspects,
Of many marvelous ornaments,
Of marvelous and many uplifted weapons;

Wearing marvelous garlands and garments,
With marvelous perfumes and ointments,
Made up of all wonders, the god,
Infinite, with faces in all directions.

Of a thousand suns in the sky
If suddenly should burst forth
The light, it would be like
Unto the light of that exalted one.

Arjuna said:

I see the gods in Thy body, O God,
All of them, and the hosts of various kinds of beings too,
Lord Brahmā sitting on the lotus-seat,
And the seers all, and the divine serpents.

With many arms, bellies, mouths, and eyes,
I see Thee, infinite in form on all sides;
No end nor middle nor yet beginning of Thee
Do I see, O All-God, All-formed!

With diadem, club, and disc,
A mass of radiance, glowing on all sides,
I see Thee, hard to look at, on every side
With the glory of flaming fire and sun, immeasurable.

Thou art the Imperishable, the supreme Object of Knowledge;
Thou art the ultimate resting-place of this universe;
Thou art the immortal guardian of the eternal right,
Thou art the everlasting Spirit, I hold.

Without beginning, middle, or end, of infinite power,
Of infinite arms, whose eyes are the moon and sun,
I see Thee, whose face is flaming fire,
Burning this whole universe with Thy radiance.

For this region between heaven and earth
Is pervaded by Thee alone, and all the directions;
Seeing this Thy wondrous, terrible form,
The triple world trembles, O exalted one!

Homage be to Thee from in front and from behind,
Homage be to Thee from all sides, Thou All!
O Thou of infinite might, Thy prowess is unmeasured;
Thou attainest all; therefore Thou art All!

Thou art the father of the world of things that move and move not,
And Thou art its revered, most venerable Guru;
There is no other like Thee—how then a greater?—
Even, in the three worlds, O Thou of matchless greatness!

Therefore, bowing and prostrating my body,
I beg grace of Thee, the Lord to be revered:
As a father to his son, as a friend to his friend,
As a lover to his beloved, be pleased to show mercy, O God!

Having seen what was never seen before, I am thrilled,
And at the same time my heart is shaken with fear;
Show me, O God, that same form of Thine as before!
Be merciful, Lord of Gods, Abode of the World!

Wearing the diadem, carrying the club, with disc in hand,
Just as before I desire to see Thee;
In that same four-armed shape
Present Thyself, O Thousand-armed One, of universal form!

The Blessed One said:

This form that is right hard to see,
Which thou hast seen of Mine,
Of this form even the gods
Constantly long for the sight.

Not by the Vedas nor by austerity,
Nor by gifts or acts of worship,
Can I be seen in such a guise,
As thou hast seen Me.

But by unanswering devotion can
I in such a guise, Arjuna,
Be known and seen in very truth,
And entered into, scorcher of the foe.

Doing My work, intent on Me,
Devoted to Me, free from attachment,

Free from enmity to all beings,
Who is so, goes to Me, son of Pâṇḍu.[12]
(11.10–12, 15–20, 40, 43–46, 52–55)

3. *The Perfect Yogin*

When the thought, controlled,
Settles on the Self alone,
The man free from longing for all desires
Is then called disciplined.

As a lamp stationed in a windless place
Flickers not, this image is recorded
Of the disciplined man controlled in thought,
Practising discipline of the Self.

When the thought comes to rest,
Checked by the practice of discipline,
And when, the Self by the self
Contemplating, he finds satisfaction in the Self;

That supernal bliss which
Is to be grasped by the consciousness and is beyond the senses,
When he knows this, and not in the least
Swerves from the truth, abiding fixed in it;

And which having gained, other gain
He counts none higher than it;
In which established, by no misery,
However grievous, is he moved;

This state, let him know,—from conjunction with misery
The disjunction,—is known as discipline;
With determination must be practised this
Discipline, with heart undismayed.

The desires that spring from purposes
Abandoning, all without remainder,
With the thought-organ alone the throng of senses
Restraining altogether,

Little by little let him come to rest
Thru the consciousness, held with firmness;
Keeping the thought-organ fixed in the Self,
He should think on nothing at all.

Because of whatsoever thing strays
The thought-organ, fickle and unstable,
From every such thing holding it back,
He shall bring it into control in the Self alone.

For to him when his thought-organ is tranquil,
To the disciplined one, supreme bliss
Approaches, his passion stilled,
Become one with Brahman, stainless.

Thus ever disciplining himself,
The disciplined man, free from stain,
Easily to contact with Brahman,
To endless bliss, attains.

Himself as in all beings,
And all beings in himself,
Sees he whose Self is disciplined in discipline,
Who sees the same in all things.

Who sees Me in all,
And sees all in Me,
For him I am not lost,
And he is not lost for Me.

Me as abiding in all beings whose
Reveres, adopting the belief in one-ness,
The abiding in any possible condition,
That disciplined man abides in Me.

By comparison with himself, in all beings
Whoso sees the same, Arjuna,
Whether it be pleasure or pain,
He is deemed the supreme disciplined man.[12]

(*Ibid.*, 6.18–32)

4. *Strive for Wisdom*

Fearlessness, singleness of soul, the will
Always to strive for wisdom; opened hand
And governed appetites; and piety
And love of lonely study; humbleness,
Uprightness, heed to injure nought which lives,
Truthfulness, slowness unto wrath, a mind
That lightly letteth go what others prize;
And equanimity, and charity
Which spieth no man's faults; and tenderness
Towards all that suffer; a contented heart,
Fluttered by no desires; a bearing mild,
Modest, and grave, with manhood nobly mixed
With patience, fortitude, and purity;
An unrevengeful spirit, never given
To rate itself too high;—such be the signs,
O Indian Prince! of him whose feet are set
On that fair path which leads to heavenly birth!

Deceitfulness, and arrogance, and pride,
Quickness to anger, harsh and evil speech,
And ignorance, to its own darkness blind,—
These be the signs, My Prince! of him whose birth
Is fated for the regions of the vile.[13]

IX. The *Mahā-Bhārata*

The "Great Story of the War of the Bhāratas" is a huge epic poem of 90,000 double verses. It describes the ruthless rivalry which separates the two lines of descendants of Bhārata, the hundred Kauravas, on the one hand, and their cousins, the five Pāṇḍavas, on the other. The Pāṇḍavas are victorious at the end of a general carnage which leads ultimately to their own death (No. 2 below).

The narration is interrupted here and there by related episodes, by fables and apologues, or by political and moral dissertations which transform this long poem into a kind of résumé of the principal values of Hinduism, a résumé, however, which allots more space to the *dharma* of the warrior than to that of a Brahmin or an ascetic.

The authors of the *Mahā-Bhārata* cannot be individualized. Its redaction may be placed sometime between the second or third century B.C. and the first century A.D.

Nos. 3 and 4 below describe the respective opinions of Draupadī, common wife of the Pāṇḍavas, and of Yudhisthira, the Pāṇḍava chief, on the events which brought about their misfortune, and on the lessons which should be derived from them.

1. *On the Origin and Value of the Four Castes*

Brahmā thus formerly created the Brâhmanic Prajāpatis,[a] penetrated by his own energy, and in splendour equalling the sun and fire. The lord then formed truth, righteousness, austere fervour, and the eternal Veda, virtuous practice, and purity for the attainment of heaven. He also formed the gods, demons and men, Brahmins, Kṣatriyas, Vaiśyas, and Śūdras, as well as all other classes of beings. The colour of the Brahmins was white; that of the Kṣatriyas red; that of the Vaiśyas yellow, and that of the Śūdras black.

If the caste of the four classes is distinguished by their colour, then a confusion of all the castes is observable. Desire, anger, fear, cupidity, grief, apprehension, hunger, fatigue, prevail over us all: by what, then, is caste discriminated? Sweat, urine, excrement, phlegm, bile, and blood are common to all; the bodies of all decay; by what, then, is caste discriminated? There are innumerable kinds of things moving and stationary; how is the class of these various objects to be determined?

There is no difference of castes: this world, having been at first created by Brahmā entirely Brâhmanic, became afterwards separated into castes in consequence of works. Those Brahmins, who were fond of sensual pleasure, fiery, irascible, prone to violence, who had forsaken their duty, and were red-limbed, fell into the condition of Kṣatriyas. Those Brahmins, who derived their livelihood from kine, who were yellow, who subsisted by agriculture, and who neglected to practise their duties, entered into the state of Vaiśyas. Those Brahmins, who were addicted to mischief and falsehood, who were covetous, who lived by all kinds of work, who were black and had fallen from purity, sank into the condition of Śūdras. Being separated from each other by these works, the Brahmins became divided into different castes. Duty and the rites of sacrifice have not been always forbidden to any of them. Such are the four classes for whom the Brâhmanic Sarasvatī[b] was at first designed by Brahmā, but who thought their cupidity fell into ignorance. Brahmins live agreeably to the prescriptions of the Veda; while they continually hold fast the Veda, and observances, and ceremonies, their austere fervour does not perish. And sacred science was created the highest thing: they who are ignorant of it are no twice-born men. Of these there are various other classes in different places, who have lost all knowledge sacred and profane, and practise whatever observances they please. And different sorts of creatures with the purificatory rites of Brahmins, and discerning their own duties, are created by different Ṛṣis[c] through their own austere fervour. This creation, sprung from the primal god, having its root in *brāhman,* undecaying, imperishable, is called the mind-born creation, and is devoted to the prescriptions of duty.

What is that in virtue of which a man is a Brahmin, a Kṣatriya, a Vaiśya, or a Śūdra; tell me, o most eloquent Ṛṣi.

He who is pure, consecrated by the natal and other ceremonies, who has completely studied the Veda, lives in the practice of the six ceremonies, performs perfectly the rites of purification, who eats the remains of oblations, is attached to his religious teacher, is constant in religious observances, and devoted to truth,—is called a Brahmin. He in whom are seen truth, liberality, inoffensiveness, harmlessness, modesty, compassion, and austere fervour,—is declared to be a Brahmin. He who practises the duty arising out of the kingly office, who is addicted to the study of the Veda, and who delights in giving and receiving,—is called a Kṣatriya. He who readily occupies himself with cattle, who is devoted to agriculture and acquisition, who is pure, and is perfect in the study of the Veda,—is denominated a Vaiśya. He who is habitually addicted to all kinds of food, performs all kinds of work, who is unclean, who has abandoned the Veda, and does not practise pure observances,—is traditionally called a Śūdra. And this which I have stated is the mark of a Śūdra, and it is not found in a Brahmin: such a Śūdra will remain a Śūdra, while the Brahmin who so acts will be no Brahmin.[14]

[a] Secondary gods, considered as emanating from Brahman.
[b] The goddess of speech.
[c] Primitive seers.

2. *The Renunciation of Their Kingdom by the Five Sons of Pāṇḍu and Their Journey Towards Indra's Heaven in the Mountain Meru*

When the four brothers knew the high resolve of king Yudhiṣṭhira,
Forthwith with Draupadī[a] they issued forth, and after them a dog
Followed: the king himself went out the seventh from the royal city,
And all the citizens and women of the palace walked behind;
But none could find it in their heart to say unto the king, "Return."
And so at length the train of citizens went back, bidding adieu.

Then the high-minded sons of Pāṇḍu and the noble Draupadī
Roamed onwards, fasting, with their faces towards the east; their hearts
Yearning for union with the Infinite; bent on abandonment
Or worldly things. They wandered on to many countries, many a sea
And river. Yudhiṣṭhira walked in front, and next to him came Bhīma,
And Arjuna came after him, and then, in order, the twin brothers.
And last of all came Draupadī, with her dark skin and lotus-eyes—
The faithful Draupadī, loveliest of women, best of noble wives—
Behind them walked the only living thing that shared their pilgrimage—
The dog—and by degrees they reached the briny sea. There Arjuna
Cast in the waves his bow and quivers. Then with souls well-disciplined
They reached the northern region, and beheld with heaven-aspiring hearts
The mighty mountain Himavant.[b] Beyond its lofty peak they passed
Towards a sea of sand, and saw at last the rocky Meru, king
Of mountains. As with eager steps they hastened on, their souls intent
On union with the Eternal, Draupadī lost hold of her high hope,
And faltering fell upon the earth.

[One by one the others also drop, till only Bhīma, Yudhiṣṭhira, and the dog are left.

Still Yudhiṣṭhira walks steadily in front, calm and unmoved, looking neither to the right hand nor to the left, and gathering up his soul in inflexible resolution. Bhīma, shocked at the fall of his companions, and unable to understand how beings so apparently guileless should be struck down by fate, appeals to his brother, who, without looking back, explains that death is the consequence of sinful thoughts and to great attachment to worldly objects; and that Draupadī's fall was owing to her excessive affection for Arjuna; Sahadeva's (who is supposed to be the most humble-minded of the five brothers) to his pride in his own knowledge; Nakula's (who is very handsome) to feelings of personal vanity; and Arjuna's to a boastful confidence in his power to destroy his foes. Bhīma then feels himself falling, and is told that he suffers death for his selfishness, pride, and too great love of enjoyment.

The sole survivor is now Yudhiṣṭhira, who still walks steadily forward, followed only by the dog.]

When with a sudden sound that rang through earth and heaven the mighty god
Came towards him in a chariot, and he cried, "Ascend, o resolute prince,"
Then did the king look back upon his fallen brothers, and address'd
These words unto the Thousand-eyed[c] in anguish—"Let my brothers here
Come with me. Without them, O god of gods, I would never wish to enter
E'en heaven; and yonder tender princess Draupadī, the faithful wife,
Worthy of endless bliss, let her too come. In mercy hear my prayer."

[Upon this, Indra informs him that the spirits of Draupadī and his brothers are already in heaven, and that he alone is permitted to ascend there in bodily form. Yudhiṣṭhira now stipulates that his dog shall be permitted with him. Indra says sternly, "Heaven has no place for men accompanied by dogs"; but Yudhiṣṭhira is unshaken in his resolution, and declines abandoning the faithful animal. Indra remonstrates—"You have abandoned your brothers and Draupadī; why not forsake the dog?" To this Yudhiṣṭhira haughtily replies, "I had no power to bring them back to life: how can there be abandonment of those who no longer live?"

The dog, it appears, is his own father Dharma[d] in disguise. Reassuming now his proper form, he praises Yudhiṣṭhira for his constancy, and they enter heaven together. There, to his surprise, he finds Duryodhana[e] and his cousins, but not his brothers or Draupadī. Hereupon he declines remaining in heaven without them. An angel is then sent to conduct him to the lower regions and across the Vaitaraṇī[f] to the hell where they are supposed to be.

The particular hell to which Yudhiṣṭhira is taken is a dense wood, whose leaves are sharp swords, and its ground paved with razors. The way to it is strewed with foul and mutilated corpses. Hideous shapes flit across the air and hover over him. Here there is an awful sensation of palpable darkness. There the wicked are burning in flames of blazing fire. Suddenly he hears the voices of his brothers and companions imploring him to assuage their torments, and not desert them. His resolution is taken. Deeply affected, he bids the angel leave him to share their miseries. This is his last trial. The whole scene now vanishes. It was a mere illusion, to test his constancy to the utmost. He is now directed to bathe in the heavenly Ganges; and having plunged into the sacred stream, he enters the real heaven, where at length, in company with

Draupadī and his brothers, he finds that rest and happiness which were unattainable on earth.][15]

(17.24 ff.)

[a] The common wife of the five brothers, the Pāṇḍavas (sons of Pāṇḍu).
[b] The Himalayas.
[c] God Indra, king of the old pantheon.
[d] The law personified.
[e] The chief of the Kauravas.
[f] The river which flows between earth and the lower regions, the Hindū Styx.

3. *The Tyranny of the Divinity*

O monarch, impelled by a perverse sense during that dire hour of a losing match at dice, thou didst yet stake and lose thy kingdom, thy wealth, thy weapons, thy brothers, and myself!

Simple, gentle, liberal, modest, truthful, how, O King, could thy mind be attracted to the vice of gambling? I am almost deprived of my sense, O King, and my heart is overwhelmed with grief, beholding this thy distress, and this thy calamity! An old history is cited as an illustration for the truth that men are subjects to the will of God and never to their own wishes! The Supreme Lord and Ordainer of all ordaineth everything in respect of the weal and woe, the happiness and misery, of all creatures, even prior to their births, guided by the acts of each, which are even like a seed destined to sprout forth.

O hero amongst men, as a wooden doll is made to move its limbs by the wire-puller, so are creatures made to work by the Lord of all. O Bhārata, like space that covereth every object, God, pervading every creature, ordaineth its weal or woe. Like a bird tied with a string, every creature is dependent on God. Every one is subject to God and none else. No one can be his own ordainer. Like a pearl on its string, or a bull held fast by the cord passing through its nose, or a tree fallen from the bank into the middle of the stream, every creature followeth the command of the Creator, because imbued with His Spirit and because established in Him. And man himself, dependent on the Universal Soul, cannot pass a moment independently.

Enveloped in darkness, creatures are not masters of their own weal or woe. They go to heaven or hell urged by God Himself. Like light straws dependent on strong winds, all creatures, O Bhārata, are dependent on God! And God Himself, pervading all creatures and engaged in acts right and wrong, moveth in the universe, though none can say "This is God." This body with its physical attributes is only the means by which God maketh every creature to reap fruits that are good or bad.

Behold the power of illusion that hath been spread by God, who confounding with his illusion, maketh creatures slay their fellows!

Truth-knowing sages behold these differently. They appear to them in a different light, even like the rays of the Sun. Ordinary men behold the things of the earth otherwise. It is God who maketh them all, adopting different processes in their creation and destruction.

And, O Yudhiṣṭhira, the Selfcreate Grandsire, Almighty God, spreading illusion, slayeth his creatures by the instrumentality of his creatures, as one may break a piece of inert and senseless wood with wood, or stone with stone, or iron with iron! And the Supreme Lord, according to his pleasure, sporteth with his creatures, creating and destroying them, like a child with his toy.

O King, it doth seem to me that God behaveth towards his creatures like a father or mother unto them. Like a vicious person, He seemeth to bear himself towards them in anger! Beholding superior and well-behaved and modest persons persecuted, while the sinful are happy, I am sorely troubled!

Beholding this thy distress and the prosperity of Suyodhana, I do not speak highly the Great Ordainer who suffereth such inequality! Or sir, what fruits doth the Great Ordainer reap by granting prosperity to Dhṛtarāṣṭra's son who transgresseth the ordinances, who is crooked and covetous, and who injureth virtue and religion!

If the act done pursueth the doer and none else, then certainly it is God himself who is stained with the sin of every act. If, however, the sin of an act done doth not attach to the doer, then individual might is the true cause of acts, and I grieve for those that have no might![16]

(3.30)

4. *Praise of Virtue*

Thy speech, O Yājñasenī,[a] is delightful, smooth and full of excellent phrases. We have listened to it. Thou speakest, however, the language of atheism!

O princess, I never act, solicitous of the fruits of my actions! I give away, because it is my duty to give; I sacrifice, because it is my duty to sacrifice! O Kṛṣṇa, I accomplish to the best of my power whatever a person living in domesticity should do, regardless of the fact whether those acts have fruits or not. O thou of fair hips, I act virtuously, not from the desire of reaping the fruits of virtue, but of not transgressing the ordinances of the Veda, and beholding also the conduct of the good and wise!

My heart, O Kṛṣṇa, is naturally attracted towards virtue. The man who wisheth to reap the fruits of virtue is a trader in virtue. His nature is mean and he should never be counted amongst the virtuous, nor doth he ever obtain the fruits of his virtues! Nor doth he of sinful heart, who having accomplished a virtuous act doubteth in his mind, obtain the fruits of his act, in consequence of that scepticism of his! I speak unto thee, under the authority of the Vedas, which constitute the highest proof in such matters, that never shouldst thou doubt virtue! The man of weak understanding who doubteth religion, virtue or the words of the Seers, is precluded from regions of immortality and bliss.

O daughter of Draupadī, religion is the only raft for those desirous of going to heaven, like a ship to merchants desirous of crossing the ocean. O thou faultless one, if the virtues that are practised by the virtuous had no fruits, this universe then would be enveloped in infamous darkness. No one then would pursue salvation, no one would seek to acquire knowledge, not even wealth, but men would live like beasts. If asceticism, the austerities of celebate life, sacrifices, study of the Vedas, charity, honesty,—these all were fruitless, men would not have practised virtues generation after generation. If acts were all fruitless, a dire confusion would ensure. For what then do Seers and gods and Gāndharvas and Rākṣasas,[b] who are all independent of human conditions, cherish virtue with such affection? Knowing it for certain that God is the giver of fruits in respect of virtue, they practise virtue in this world. This, O Kṛṣṇa, is the eternal source of prosperity!

Therefore, though you mayest not see the fruits of virtue, thou shouldst not yet doubt religion or the gods. Thou must perform sacrifices with a will, and practise charity without insolence. Acts in this world have their fruits, and virtue also is eternal.

Let thy doubt, therefore, O Kṛṣṇa, be dispelled like mist. Reflecting upon all this, let thy scepticism give way to faith. Slander not God, who is the lord of all creatures. Learn how to know Him. Bow down unto Him. Let not thy mind be such. And, O Kṛṣṇa, never disregard that Supreme Being through whose grace, mortal man by piety, acquireth immortality![17]

(3.30)

[a] Another name of Kṛṣṇa, or Draupadī.
[b] Demigods and demons.

5. *The Serpent Sacrifice*

When King Janamejaya had learnt from his ministers the ghastly tale of his father's death he resolved to take revenge upon Takṣaka[a] and his tribe. He vowed that he would celebrate a serpent sacrifice, and inquired from his priests whether they knew any rite by which Takṣaka could be compelled to throw himself in the sacrificial fire. The Brahmins answered him that they did know the rites of the serpent sacrifice which of old had been instituted by the gods for the sake of the King himself and which could be performed by him alone. Then King Janamejaya deemed his revenge certain, and ordered the sacrificial implements to be brought.

The priests, after measuring off the place for sacrifice as prescribed in the ritual, consecrated the King so that he might gain the desired object of the oblation. But while the *sūtra-dhāra*[b] was preparing the place of sacrifice, he noticed certain signs which betokened that the great rite would not be brought to an end owing to the interference by a Brahmin. The King, therefore, issued strict orders to the doorkeeper that on no account was any unknown person to be admitted. Now the priests proceeded to perform the rites of the serpent sacrifice, and, when they had kindled the sacrificial fire, the snakes were seized with terror. Compelled by the powerful spell, the serpents came from every side, quivering and hissing and curling round one another with head and tail, and hurled themselves into the blazing flames. They were white, black, and dark blue, old and young, and they produced sounds of various kinds. Some were a mile in length, others not larger than a cow's ear. Some were swift like steeds, and others huge-bodied like unto elephants. In hundreds and thousands, in myriads and millions, they were drawn irresistibly towards the fire, in which they found a certain death. Thus the curse pronounced upon her disobedient sons by Kadrū, the Mother of Snakes, was fulfilled.

Now Takṣaka, as soon as he learnt that King Janamejaya had been consecrated for the sacrifice, had sought shelter in the abode of Indra. He entreated the chief of the gods[c] to afford him protection and to save him from destruction. Indra spake to him: "Thou needest not be afraid, O Takṣaka, Lord of Snakes, of this serpent sacrifice. Brahmā hath been propitiated by me before on thy behalf; therefore thou needest not fear. Dispel the fever from thy mind."

Thus comforted, the best of snakes dwelt joyfully in the abode of Indra. But the Serpent King Vāsuki was seized with dismay and grief, when he saw his retinue steadily waning, as the Nāgas were tumbling incessantly into the sacrificial flames. Fear fell upon him, and with trembling heart he spoke to his sister: "My limbs, O fair one, are burning, and I distinguish no longer the regions of the sky. I sink under the burden of bewilderment and my heart quaketh. My sight wandereth sorely and my heart is torn asunder. Now, truly, shall I too fall unwillingly into the blazing fire. For this sacrifice of Parikṣit's son[d] is held because the King strives after our destruction. Surely I, too, shall have to go to the abode of the Lord of the Dead.[e] Now the occasion hath come wherefore thou, my sister, hast been betrothed by me to Jaratkāru. Save us and our kin. Āstīka, indeed, O thou best among serpent-dames, will ward off this holocaust. So Brahmā himself hath told me. Therefore, beloved sister, speak thou to thy dear son, who, though young in years, is honoured by the aged, and entreat him, who knoweth the Veda well, for the deliverance of me and my servants."

Then Jaratkāru, the sister of the serpent king, summoned her son and told him how Kadrū had cursed her children, and how she herself had been given in marriage to the hermit Jaratkāru so that her son born from their union might save the Nāgas from dire destruction. This Brahmā himself had declared when, after the churning of the ocean, Vāsuki had begged the gods for their protection as a reward for his help in the winning of the nectar. Thus called upon now to fulfil that purpose of her marriage, her son, Āstīka, at once consented. He went to his maternal uncle and, imparting to him, as it were, new life, he spake to him: "I shall save thee, O Vāsuki, Chief of Serpents, from that curse, O great being. It is the truth that I am speaking to thee. Be thou of good comfort, O Nāga; for thou needest not be afraid. I shall strive, O King, that thou mayest gain bliss. My voice hath never uttered an untruth, even when I have spoken without restraint, far less in serious matters. I shall go to King Janamejaya, who hath been consecrated for the sacrifice, and I shall propitiate him with auspicious words, O my uncle, so that the sacrifice of the King may cease. Put thy faith wholly in me, O Lord of Snakes, great in understanding; thy mind will not be disappointed in me." In this manner Āstīka comforted his uncle, while taking on himself the fever of his heart. Then he went quickly and reached the place of Janamejaya's great sacrifice, which was full of priests, resembling the sun in splendour. But when he wished to enter he was kept back by the doorkeepers. Then Āstīka extolled the king of unbounded glory, he lauded the sacrificing priests and the other Brahmins who were present, and, last of all, he praised Agni, the god of Fire. King Janamejaya he extolled above all the ancient rulers of the earth who had made themselves famous by their hecatombs.

Highly pleased by Āstīka's praise, the King spake to the assembled Brahmins: "Although a youth, this one speaketh like an old man; not a youth, but an old man he is deemed by me. I wish to give him a boon; concede it to me, O ye priests." But the sacrificing priests declared that a Brahmin, though he be young, must indeed be honoured by kings, yet first of all Takṣaka must be compelled to approach the fire. When they informed the King that Takṣaka had sought shelter in the abode of Indra, and that the god had promised him protection, Janamejaya, incensed in wrath, urged them to cause not only Takṣaka but Indra himself to fall in the sacrificial fire. Induced by the royal word, the sacrificers exerted themselves to the utmost and used their most powerful spells. Then Indra himself, mounted on his celestial chariot, appeared in the sky, praised by all the gods and followed by thunder-clouds and by spirits of the air and hosts of heavenly nymphs. Takṣaka had concealed himself within the folds of Indra's mantle, and trembled with fear. The priests again cited the Nāga by means of their powerful charms. Even Indra, seeing that holocaust, was seized by terror, and, leaving Takṣaka to his fate, he returned to his celestial abode. When Indra had gone, Takṣada, senseless with fear, was drawn irresistibly by the power of the *mantras*[f] towards the blazing flames.

The priests spake to the King: "Here cometh Takṣaka

speedily into thy power, O King. The mighty roar is heard of him roaring with terrifying sound. Abandoned by the Bearer of the Thunderbolt,[g] verily the Nāga tumbleth from the celestial vault, his body dropping by the magic spells. Whirling through the air, he cometh bereft of his senses, the Lord of Snakes, hissing his violent hissings."

Now King Janamejaya, deeming his aim fulfilled, spake to Āstīka: "O worthy youth, I grant thee a boon deserving of thy unbounded greatness. Choose, and whatsoever wish there dwelleth in thy heart I will give it thee, even though it were ungivable." Then, at the very moment when Takṣaka was about to fall in the fire, Āstīka answered: "If thou givest me a boon, it is this I choose, O Janamejaya. Let this thy sacrifice cease, and may the snakes be saved." Upon these words the son of Parikṣit, not overpleased, said to Āstīka: "Gold, silver, and kine and whatsoever else thou likest, let me give thee that as a boon, O youth, but let not my sacrifice cease." Āstīka answered: "Gold, silver, and kine I do not choose from thee, O King. May this thy sacrifice cease: hail to the race of our mother." In vain the King endeavoured to persuade Āstīka to choose some other boon, until at last the assembled priests advised the King: "Let the Brahmin attain his wish." Thus Takṣaka was saved.[18]

(1.49–58)

[a] The lord of snakes.
[b] The architect of the sacrificial altar.
[c] Indra.
[d] Janamejaya.
[e] God Yama.
[f] Sacred formulas.
[g] Indra.

6. *The Man in the Well*

A Brahmin loses his way in a dense forest full of beasts of prey. In great terror he runs here and there, looking in vain for a way out. Then he sees that the terrible forest is surrounded on all sides by traps and is embraced by both arms of a dreadful-looking woman. Great and terrible five-headed dragons, which reach up like rocks to the sky, surround this great forest. And in the middle of this forest, covered by underwood and creeping plants, there is a well. The Brahmin falls into it and is caught on the intertwined branches of a creeper. As the great fruit of a bread-fruit tree, held by its stalks, hangs down, so he hung there, feet upwards, head downwards. And yet another even greater danger threatens him there. In the middle of the well he perceived a great, mighty dragon, and at the edge of the lid of the well he saw a black, six-mouthed and twelve-footed giant elephant slowly approaching. In the branches of the tree which covered the well, swarmed all kinds of dreadful-looking bees, preparing honey. The honey drips down and is greedily drunk by the man hanging in the well. For he was not weary of existence, and did not give up hope of life, though white and black mice gnawed the tree on which he hung. The forest is the *saṃsāra*, existence in the world: the beasts of prey are the diseases, the hideous giantess is old age, the well is the body of beings, the dragon at the bottom of the well is time, the creepers in which the man was caught, the hope of life, the six-mouthed and twelve-footed elephant, the year with six seasons and twelve months: the mice are the days and nights, and the drops of honey are sensual enjoyments.[19]

(11.5)

X. The *Rāmāyaṇa*

The "Story of Rāma," an epic in 24,000 double verses, is the work of Vālmīki, who found its elements in a rich pan-Indian legend which contained themes of folklore and perhaps also certain prehistorical reminiscences. It is the story of the adventures of prince Rāma (Rāmacandra), son of Daśaratha, and of his noble wife Sītā from the time of their exile to their triumphal return to Ayodhyā, after which there follows an unjust repudiation and the death of Sītā.

The main story lends itself to digressions. Some of these, if linked together, would form a code of Hindu conduct and morals. Although it presents from many points of view, in its composition and its contents, the courtly and polished India of later times, the work is probably to be dated near the redaction of the *Mahā-Bhārata.*

1. *A Deed of Blood committed by King Daśaratha Accidentally in His Youthful Days*

(Thus it happened):
One day when rains refreshed the earth, and caused my heart to swell with joy,
When, after scorching with his rays the parched ground, the summer sun
Had passed towards the south; when cooling breezes chased away the heat,
And grateful clouds arose; when frogs and pea-fowl sported, and the deer
Seemed drunk with glee, and all the winged creation, dripping as if drowned,
Plumed their dank feathers on the tops of wind-rocked trees, and falling showers
Covered the mountains till they looked like watery heaps, and torrents poured
Down from their sides, filled with loose stones and red as dawn with mineral earth,
Winding like serpents in their course; then at that charming season I,
Longing to breathe the air, went forth, with bow and arrow in my hand,
To seek for game, if haply by the river-side a buffalo

Or elephant or other animal might cross, at eve, my path,
Coming to drink. Then in the dusk I heard the sound of gurgling water:
Quickly I took my bow, and aiming toward the sound, shot off the dart.
A cry of mortal agony came from the spot,—a human voice
Was heard, and a poor hermit's son fell pierced and bleeding in the stream.
"Ah! wherefore then," he cried, "am I a harmless hermit's son struck down?
Hither to this lone brook I came at eve to fill my water-jar.
By whom have I been smitten? whom have I offended? Oh! I grieve
Not for myself or my own fate, but for my parents, old and blind,
Who perish in my death. Ah! what will be the end of that loved pair,
Long guided and supported by my hand? this barbed dart has pierced
Both me and them." Hearing that piteous voice, I Daśaratha,
Who meant no harm to any human creature, young or old, became
Palsied with fear; my bow and arrows dropped from my senseless hands;
And I approached the place in horror; there with dismay I saw,
Stretched on the bank, an innocent hermit-boy, writhing in pain and smeared
With dust and blood, his knotted hair dishevelled, and a broken jar
Lying beside him. I stood petrified and speechless. He on me
Fixed full his eyes, and then, as if to burn my inmost soul, he said,
"How have I wronged thee, monarch? that thy cruel hand has smitten me—
Me, a poor hermit's son, born in the forest: father, mother, child

Hast thou transfixed with this one arrow: they, my parents, sit at home
Expecting my return, and long will cherish hope—a prey to thirst
And agonizing fears. Go to my father—tell him of my fate,
Lest his dread curse consume thee, as the flame devours the withered wood.
But first in pity draw thou forth the shaft that pierces to my heart,
And checks the gushing life-blood, as the bank obstructs the bounding stream."
He ceased, and as he rolled his eyes in agony, and quivering writhed
Upon the ground, I slowly drew the arrow from the poor boy's side.
Then with a piteous look, his features set in terror, he expired.
Distracted at the grievous crime, wrought by my hand unwittingly;
Sadly I thought within myself, how best I might repair the wrong.
Then took the way he had directed me towards the hermitage.
There I beheld his parents, old and blind; like two clipped wingless birds
Sitting forlorn, without their guide, awaiting his arrival anxiously,
And, to beguile their weariness, conversing of him tenderly.
Quickly they caught the sound of footsteps, and I heard the old man say,
With chiding voice, "Why hast thou lingered, child? Quick give us both to drink
A little water. Long forgetful of us, in the cooling stream
Hast thou disported; come in—for thy mother yearneth for her son.
If she or I in ought have caused thee pain, or spoken hasty words,
Think on thy hermit's duty of forgiveness; bear them not in mind.

Thou art the refuge of us refugeless—the eyes of thy blind sire.
Why art thou silent? Speak! Bound up in thee are both thy parents' lives."
He ceased, and I stood paralysed—till by an effort resolutely
Collecting all my powers of utterance, with faltering voice I said,
"Pious and noble hermit; I am not thy son; I am the king:
Wandering with bow and arrow by a stream, seeking for game, I pierced
Unknowingly thy child. The rest I need not tell. Be gracious to me."
Hearing my pitiless words, announcing his bereavement, he remained
Senseless awhile; then drawing a deep sigh, his face all bathed in tears,
He spake to me as I approached him suppliantly, and slowly said,
"Hadst thou not come thyself, to tell the awful tale, its load of guilt
Had crushed thy head into ten thousand fragments. This ill-fated deed
Was wrought by thee unwittingly, O King, else hadst thou not been spared,
And all the race of Rāghavas had perished. Lead us to the place:
All bloody though he be, and lifeless, we must look upon our son
For the last time, and clasp him in our arms." Then weeping bitterly
The pair, led by my hand, came to the spot and fell upon their son.
Thrilled by the touch, the father cried, "My child, hast thou no greeting for us?
No word of recognition: wherefore liest thou here upon the ground?
Are thou offended? or am I no longer loved by thee, my son?

See here thy mother. Thou wert ever dutiful towards us both.
Why wilt thou not embrace me? speak one tender word. Whom shall I hear
Reading again the sacred Śâstra in the early morning hours?
Who now will bring me roots and fruits to feed me like a cherished guest?
How, weak and blind, can I support thy aged mother, pining for her son?
Stay! Go not yet to Death's abode—stay with thy parents yet one day,
To-morrow we will both go with thee on the dreary way. Forlorn
And sad, deserted by our child, without protector in the wood,
Soon shall we both depart toward the mansions of the King of death."
Thus bitterly lamenting, he performed the funeral rites; then turning
Towards me thus addressed me, standing reverently near—"I had
But this one child, and thou hast made me childless. Now strike down
The father: I shall feel no pain in death. But thy requital be
That sorrow for a child shall one day bring thee also to the grave."[20]

(2.63)

2. *Condition of Mortality*

In scatterings end collections all;
High towering piles at length must fall;
In parting every meeting ends;
To death all life of creatures tends.
The early fall to earth is sure,
Of fruits on trees that hang mature.
Of mortals here behold a type;
They, too, succumb, for death when ripe.
As houses fall when long decay
Has worn the posts which formed their stay,

So sink men's frames, when age's course
Has undermined their vital force.
The nights which once have passed away,
And mingled with the morning ray,
Return no more,—as streams which blend
With ocean, there for ever end.
Revolving ceaseless, night and day,
The lives of mortals wear away;
As summer's torrid solar beams
Dry up the ever lessening streams.
In hours when men at home abide,
Death, too, reposes by their side;
When forth they issue, day by day,
Death walks companion of their way;
Death with them goes when far they roam;
Death with them stays, death brings them home.
Men hail the rising sun with glee,
They love his setting glow to see,
But fail to mark that every day
In fragments bears their life away.
All nature's face delight to view,
As changing seasons come anew;
Few see how each revolving year
Abridges swiftly man's career.
As logs that on the ocean float,
By chance are into contact brought,
But, tossed about by wind and tide,
Together cannot long abide;—
So wives, sons, kinsmen, riches, all
Whate'er our own we fondly call,—
Obtained, possessed, enjoyed, to-day,
To-morrow all are snatched away.
As, standing on the road a man
Who sees a passing caravan,
Which slowly winds across the plain,
Cries, "I will follow in your train";

So men the beaten path must tread
On which their sires of yore have led.
Since none can nature's course elude,
Why o'er thy doom in sorrow brood?[21]

(2.105, 16 ff.)

XI. The *Purāṇas*

The *Purāṇas* or "Antiquities" are versified texts, each of which is, as a general rule, devoted to a description of the characteristics and exploits of some great divinity and to a statement of the elements of his related cult and the pilgrimages which are associated with it. Actually, the treatises, often voluminous, contain details on the creation of the world, the genealogy of gods, human prehistory, royal dynasties—in addition to many digressions, some concerning secular subjects, others dealing with religious or speculative matters. The *Purāṇas* originate from the beginning of our era to the tenth century and even later. Over these centuries their vast subject matter has nourished the beliefs and practices of the Hindus. There are eighteen principal *Purāṇas* and a great number of secondary *Purāṇas.*

No. 2 gives the story of the descent into hell of the king Vipaścit who for a minor fault deserved an instant of punishment. The servant of the god of death shows him human beings who are submitted to ordeals, and then invites him to leave the place of suffering. Then the miracle is produced. . . .

1. *Hymn to Caṇḍikā*

O goddess, who removest the suffering of thy suppliants, be gracious!
Be gracious, O mother of the whole world!
Be gracious, O queen of the universe; safeguard the universe!
Thou, O goddess, art queen of all that is moveable and immoveable!
Thou alone hast become the support of the world,
Because thou dost subsist in the form of the earth!
By thee, who existest in the form of water, all
This universe is filled, O thou inviolable in thy valour!
Thou art Viṣṇu's energy, boundless in thy valour;
Thou art the germ of the universe, thou art Illusion sublime!
All this world has been bewitched, O goddess;
Thou indeed when attained art the cause of final emancipation from existence on the earth!

All sciences are portions of thee, O goddess;
So are females without exception in the worlds!
By thee alone, as mother, this world has been filled!
What praise can there be for thee? Thou art beyond praise, the sublimest expression!

O goddess, be gracious! Protect us wholly from fear of our foes
Perpetually, as thou hast at this very time saved us promptly by the slaughter of the Asuras![a]
And bring thou quickly to rest the sins of all the worlds
And the great calamities which have sprung from the maturing of portents!
To us who are prostrate be thou gracious,
O goddess, who takest away affliction from the universe!
O thou worthy of praise from the dwellers in the three worlds,
Bestow thou boons on the worlds![22]

(*Caṇḍī-māhātmya*, 10)

[a] A class of demons, opponents of the gods.

2. *King Vipaścit's Visit to Hell*

Ho! servant of Yama! say, what sin have I committed, for which I have incurred this deepest hell, frightful for its torments? Known as Vipaścit, I was born in the family of the Janakas, in the country of Videha, in very truth a guardian of men. I sacrificed with many sacrifices; I protected the earth with uprightness; nor did I let fighting rage; no guest departed with averted countenance; nor did I offend the *pitṛs,*[a] the gods, the seers or my servants; nor did I covet other men's wives, or wealth, or aught else belonging to them. At the moon's changes the *pitṛs*, on other lunar days the gods, voluntarily approached mankind as cows a pool. The two religious duties, both sacrifice and meritorious work, perish inasmuch as the performers of domestic sacrifices depart sighing with averted faces. The merit amassed in seven lives is dissipated by the sighing of the *pitṛs;* the sighing assuredly destroys the destiny that springs from three lives. Hence I was ever indeed kindly disposed to what concerned the gods and the *pitṛs;* being such, how have I incurred this very terrible hell?

Yama's officer spoke:

Come then, we go elsewhere. Thou hast now seen everything, for thou hast seen hell. Come then, let us go elsewhere.

The recitant spoke:

Thereupon the king prepared to follow him; and then a cry went up from all the men that abode in torment, "Be gracious, O King! stay but a moment, for the air that clings to thy body gladdens our mind, and entirely dispels the burning and the sufferings and pains from our bodies, O tiger-like man! Be gracious, O King!"

On hearing this their entreaty, the king asked that servant of Yama—How do I afford gladness to these men? Have I done such a mighty deed of merit in the world of mortals, wherefrom falls this gladdening shower? Declare me that.

Yama's officer spoke:

Inasmuch as thy body was nourished with the food that remained, after the *pitṛs*, the gods, guests and servants were satisfied, and since thy mind was attached to them, hence the air that clings to thy body brings gladness; the torment, O King! does not hurt the evil-doers. Whereas thou didst offer the horse-sacrifice and other sacrifices according to precept, hence from seeing thee Yama's engines weapons, fires and crows, which cause intense suffering, such as crushing, cutting, burning and so forth, grow mild, O King! when counteracted by thy majesty.

The king spoke:

Neither in heaven nor in Brahmā's world do men experience such joy, methinks, as arises from conferring bliss on suffering creatures. If, while I am present, torment does not hurt these men, here then, fair Sir, I will remain firm as a mountain.

Yama's officer spoke:

Come, O King; we proceed. Enjoy the delights won by thine own merit, casting aside here the torments of evil-doers.

The king spoke:

For that reason I will not go as long as these are in sore suffering. From my near-presence the denizens of hell grow happy. Fie on the sickly protection-begging life of that man, who shews no favour to one distressed, even though he be a resolute foe! Sacrifices, gifts, austerities do not work for the welfare of him, who has no thought for the succour of the distressed. Whoever bears a cruel mind towards children, the sick and such like, and towards the aged also, I do not hold him human; he is truly a demon. But if these men have pain originating in hell, whether produced by the heat from fire, or produced by overpowering smells, and if they have the intense pain arising from hunger and thirst that causes faintness, yet the grant of deliverance to them excels, I consider, the joy of heaven. If many sufferers shall obtain happiness, while I undergo pain, should I not in truth embrace it? Go thou not therefore long.

Yama's officer spoke:

Here have both Dharma and Indra[b] arrived to lead thee

away. Thou must certainly depart from us: go therefore, O King!

Dharma spoke:

Fittingly worshipped by thee, I lead thee to heaven; mount this heavenly chariot and linger not; let us go.

The king spoke:

Men in thousands, O Dharma! suffer pain here in hell; and being in affliction they cry to me to save them; hence I depart not.

Indra spoke:

These evil-doers have come to hell in consequence of their own deeds; thou also, O King, must go to heaven in consequence of thy meritorious deed.

The king spoke:

If thou dost know, thou, O Dharma, or thou, O Indra, Śacî's lord, how great indeed is my authority, then deign to speak aright.

Dharma spoke:

Just as drops of water in the sea, or as stars in the sky, or as showers of rain, as the sands in the Ganges—just as these drops of water and other things are innumerable, O King! even so thy merit is in truth beyond reckoning. In thy evincing now this compassion here in the hells, the reckoning of that merit of thine has verily amounted to a hundred thousand. Then go, O King! enjoy then the abode of the immortals; let these also consume away in hell the sin arising from their own actions!

The king spoke:

How shall men attain their desire in things connected with me, if in my presence these people gain no prosperity. Hence, whatever good deeds I possess, O lord of the thirty gods! by means thereof let the sinners who are undergoing torment be delivered from hell!

Indra spoke:

Thus hast thou, O King! gained a more exalted station: see too these sinners delivered from hell!

The recitant spoke:

Then fell there a shower of flowers upon that king, and Hari[c] making him mount the heavenly chariot led him to the heaven-world. Both I and the others, who were there, were released from the torments; thereafter we entered the other earthly existences, as determined by the results of our own actions.[23]

(*Mārkaṇḍeya*, 13, 15)

[a] The deceased ancestors.
[b] Law personified and lord of the gods.
[c] Viṣṇu.

3. *Viṣṇu as the Highest Form of Brahman*[a]

Of that Brahman there are two conditions, one possessed of form, the other formless. These decaying and undecaying states exist in all creatures. The undecaying is the highest Brahman; the decaying is this entire universe. Just as light is diffused from a fire which is confined to one spot, so is this whole universe the diffused energy of the supreme Brahman. And as light shows a difference, greater or less, according to its nearness or distance from the fire, so is there a variation in the energy of Brahman. Brahmā, Viṣṇu and Śiva are his chief energies. The deities are inferior to them; the Yakṣas,[b] etc., to the deities; men, cattle, wild animals, birds and reptiles to the Yakṣas, etc.; and trees and plants are the lowest of all these energies. This entire universe, which, O most excellent ascetic, is subject to appearance and disappearance, to production, to destruction, and to change, is yet undecaying and eternal. Viṣṇu, containing all the energies, is the highest form of Brahman, which, at the commencement of their abstraction, is contemplated by Yogins[b] as invested with shape. Directed to him, the Great Union with its basis, and its germs, is produced in the undistracted minds of the devotees. Viṣṇu is the highest and most immediate of all the energies of Brahman, the embodied Brahman, formed of the whole of Brahman. On him this entire universe is woven and interwoven: from him is the world, and the world is in him; and he is the whole universe. Viṣṇu, the lord, consisting of what is perishable as well as what is imperishable, sustains everything, both Spirit and Matter, in the form of his ornaments and weapons.[24]

(*Viṣṇu*, 1.22, 36 ff.)

[a] Brahman as Absolute (neuter), distinguished from Brahmā (masculine), supreme god.
[b] A class of semidivine beings.

4. *The Churning of the Ocean by the Gods*

Being thus instructed by the god of gods, the divinities entered into alliance with the demons: and they jointly understood the acquirement of the beverage of immortality. They collected various kinds of medicinal herbs, and cast them into the sea of milk, the waters of which were radiant as the thin and shining clouds of autumn. Then they took the mountain Mandara for the staff, the serpent Vāsuki for the cord, and commenced to churn the ocean for the ambrosia. The assembled gods were stationed, by Kṛṣṇa, at the tail of the serpent; the Daityas and Dānavas,[a] at its head and neck, Scorched by the flames emitted from his inflated hood, the demons were shorn of their glory; whilst the clouds, driven towards his tail by the breath of his mouth, refreshed the gods with revivifying showers. In the midst of the milky sea, Hari[b] himself, in the form of a tortoise, served as a pivot for the mountain, as it was whirled around. The holder of the mace and discus[b] was present, in other forms, amongst the gods and demons, and assisted to drag the monarch of the serpent race; and, in another vast body, he sat upon the summit of the mountain. With one portion of his energy, unseen by gods and demons, he sustained the serpent-king, and, with another, infused vigour into the gods.

From the ocean, thus churned by the gods and Dānavas, first uprose the cow Surabhi, the fountain of milk and curds, worshipped by the divinities, and beheld by them and their associates with minds disturbed and eyes glistening with delight. Then, as the Saints in the sky wondered what this could be, appeared the goddess Vāruṇī,[c] her eyes rolling with intoxication. Next, from the whirlpool of the deep, sprang the Pārijāta tree,[d] the delight of nymphs of heaven; perfuming the world with its blossoms. The troop of the Apsarasas[e] were then produced, of surprising loveliness, endowed with beauty and with taste. The cool-rayed moon next rose, and was seized by Mahādeva:[f] and then poison was engendered from the sea, of which the Nāgas[g] took possession. Dhanvantari, robed in white, and bearing in his hand the cup of ambrosia, next came forth; beholding which, the sons of Diti and of Danu,[h] as well as the ascets, were filled with satisfaction and delight. Then, seated on a full-blown lotus, and holding a water-lily in her hand, the goddess Śrī,[i] radiant with beauty, rose from the waves. The great sages, enraptured, hymned her with the song dedicated to her praise, Viśvāvasu[j] and other heavenly quiristers sang, and Ghṛtācī and other celestial nymphs danced before her. Gaṅgā and other holy streams attended for her ablutions; and the elephants of the skies, taking up their pure waters in vases of gold, poured them over the goddess, the queen of the universal world. The sea of milk, in person presented her with a wreath of never-fading flowers; and the artist of the gods decorated her person with heavenly ornaments. Thus bathed, attired, and adorned, the goddess, in view of the celestials, cast herself upon the breast of Hari, and, there reclining, turned her eyes upon the deities, who were inspired with rapture by her gaze. Not so the Daityas,[k] who, with Vipracitti at their head, were filled with indignation, as Viṣṇu turned away from them: and they were abandoned by the goddess of prosperity.

The powerful and indignant Daityas then forcibly seized the cup of ambrosia that was in the hand of Dhanvantari. But Viṣṇu, assuming a female form, fascinated and deluded them, and, recovering the cup from them, delivered it to the gods. Śakra[l] and the other deities quaffed the ambrosia. The incensed demons, grasping their weapons, fell upon them. But the gods, into whom the ambrosial draught had infused new vigour, defeated and put their host to flight; and they fled through the regions of space, and plunged into the subterranean realms. The gods thereat greatly rejoiced, did homage to the holder of the discus and mace,[b] and resumed their reign in heaven. The sun shone with renovated splendour, and again discharged his appointed task; and the celestial luminaries again circled in their respective orbits. Fire once more blazed aloft, beautiful in splendour; and the minds of all beings were animated by devotion. The three worlds again were rendered happy by prosperity; and Indra, the chief of the gods, was restored to power. Seated upon his throne, and once more in heaven, exercising sovereignty over the gods, Śakra[l] eulogized the goddess who bears a lotos in her hand. Being praised, the gratified Śrī, abiding in all creatures, and heard by all beings, replied to the god of hundred rites:[l] "I am pleased, monarch of the gods, by thine adoration. Demand from me what thou desirest. I have come to fulfil thy wishes." "If, goddess," replied Indra, "thou wilt grant my prayers; if I am worthy of thy bounty; be this my first request,—that the three worlds may never again be deprived of thy presence. My second supplication, daughter of Ocean, is, that thou wilt not forsake him who shall celebrate thy praises in the words I have addressed to thee." "I will not abandon," the goddess answered, "the three worlds again. This thy first boon is granted: for I am gratified by thy praises. And, further, I will never turn my face away from that mortal who, morning and evening, shall repeat the hymn with which thou hast addressed me."[25]

(*Ibid.*, 1.9)

[a] Two classes of demons.
[b] Viṣṇu.
[c] The goddess of wine.
[d] A paradisial tree.
[e] Nymphs of heaven.
[f] Śiva.
[g] Serpent deities.
[h] Demons.
[i] Female divinity of glory and prosperity.
[j] Chief of the Gāndharvas, a class of demigods.
[k] Demons.
[l] Indra, chief of the gods.

5. *Praise of Viṣṇu's Worshippers*

"Tell me, master, how am I to distinguish the worshipper of Hari,[a] who is the protector of all beings?" Yama replied: "You are to consider the worshipper of Viṣṇu him who never deviates from the duties prescribed to his caste; who looks with equal indifference upon friend or enemy; who takes nothing, nor injures any being. Know that person of unblemished mind to be a worshipper of Viṣṇu. Know him to be a devout worshipper of Hari, who has placed Janārdana[b] in his pure mind, which has been freed from fascination, and whose soul is undefiled by the soil of the Kali age.[c] Know that excellent man to be a worshipper of Viṣṇu, who, looking upon gold in secret, holds that which is another's wealth but as grass, and devotes all his thoughts to the lord. Pure is he as a mountain of clear crystal: for how can Viṣṇu abide in the hearts of men with malice, and envy, and other evil passions? The flowing heat of fire abides not in a cluster of the cooling rays of the moon. He who lives pure in thought, free from malice, contented, leading a holy life, feeling tenderness for all creatures, speaking wisely and kindly, humble and sincere, has Vāsudeva[d] ever present in his heart.

As the young Śāla-tree, by its beauty, declares the excellence of the juices which it has imbibed from the earth, so, when the eternal has taken up his abode in the bosom of any one, that man is lovely amidst the beings of this world.

Depart quickly from those men whose sins have been dispersed by moral and spiritual merit, whose minds are daily dedicated to the imperceptible deity, and who are exempt from pride, uncharitableness, and malice.

In the heart in which the divine Hari, who is without beginning or end, abides, armed with a sword, a shell, and a mace, sin cannot remain; for it cannot coexist with that which destroys it: as darkness cannot continue in the world, when the sun is shining. The eternal makes not his abode in the heart of that man who covets another's wealth, who injures living creatures, who speaks harshness and untruth, who is proud of his iniquity, and whose mind is evil. Janārdana occupies not his thoughts who envies another's prosperity, who calumniates the virtuous, who never sacrifies, nor bestows gifts upon the pious, who is blinded by the property of darkness.

That vile wretch is no worshipper of Viṣṇu, who, through avarice, is unkind to his nearest friends and relations, to his wife, children, parents, and dependents. The brute-like man whose thoughts are evil, who is addicted to unrighteous acts, who ever seeks the society of the wicked, and suffers no day to pass without the perpetration of crime, is no worshipper of Vāsudeva.[26]

(*Ibid.*, 3.7)

[a] Viṣṇu.
[b] Viṣṇu.
[c] The evil (present) age of humanity.
[d] Viṣṇu.

XII. The *Tantras*

The *Tantras*, or the "Treatises on the Doctrine," mainly describe an often elaborated and generally symbolical ritual which characterizes those aspects of Hinduism which are called Tântrism. Like the *Purāṇas*, the *Tantras* also contain much speculation concerning rites, as well as mythical episodes which are ordinarily connected with the cult of Śakti, or "Energy," who is conceived as the wife of Śiva and as a supreme divine Being. Versified works, of which quite a number are known today, the *Tantras* were compiled at about the sixth or the seventh century.

1. *The Image of Tārā*

[Tārā is always depicted in her fearful form with four arms entwined with poisonous snakes, and serpents in her matted hair. She holds a head and a chalice, for in her fearful mood she drinks the blood, the sap of the world.]

Standing firmly with her left foot forward resting on a corpse, she laughs loudly. Transcendent, her hands hold a sword, a blue lotus, a dagger and a begging bowl. She raises her war cry: Hun! Her matted tawny hair is bound with poisonous blue snakes. Thus the terrifying Tārā destroys the unconsciousness of the three worlds and carries them on her head to the other store.

(*Tārā-tantra*)

She shines upon a white lotus arisen from the water, pervading the world. She holds in her hands scissors, a sword, a skull and a blue lotus. Her ornaments are snakes in the form of a zone, ear-rings, a garland, armlets, bracelets, anklets. She has three red eyes, fearful tawny tresses, a beautiful girdle, fearful teeth. Round the hips she wears the skin of a panther. She bears a diadem made of bleached bones. One should meditate on Tārā, the mother of the three worlds seated on the heart of a corpse, her face resplendent with the power of the Never-decaying.[27]

(*Tārā-rahasya*)

2. *The Place of Worship*

The best places are holy grounds, river banks, caves, sites of pilgrimage, the summits of mountains, confluents of rivers, sacred forests, solitary groves, the shade of the Bel tree, valleys, places overgrown with Tulsi plants, pasture lands, temples of Śiva without a bull, the foot of a sacred fig tree or of an Amalakī tree, cowsheds, islands, sanctuaries, the shore of the sea, one's own house, the abode of one's teacher, places which tend to inspire single-pointedness, lonely places free from animals.[27]

(*Gāndharva-tantra*)

3. *Purification*

The purification of the person of the worshipper consists in bathing. The purification of the subtle elements of the body is done through breath control, and through the dedication of the six main parts of the body to the six deities to which they correspond. After this are performed the other forms of dedication.

The purification of the place of worship is done by cleaning it carefully, adorning it with an auspicious ornamentation made of powders of five colours, placing a seat, a canopy, using incense, lights, flowers, garlands, etc. All this must be done by the worshipper himself.

Purification of the ritual utterances, the mantras, is done by repeating the syllables which compose them in the regular order and then in the reverse order.

Purification of the accessories is done by sprinkling water consecrated with the basic mantra and the weapon-mantra and then displaying the cow-gesture.

Purification of the deity is done by placing the image on an altar, invoking the presence of the deity through its secret mantra and the life-giving breathing-mantra, bathing the image three times while reciting the basic mantra, then adorning it with garments and jewels. After which an offering of incense and light should be made.[27]

(*Kulārṇava-tantra*)

4. *Praise of the Deity*

We cannot know a thing without knowing its merits, its qualities. All knowledge or science is based on a form of praise. A dictionary is but the praise of words. The works of science are filled with glorification. Everything which is an object of knowledge is as such a deity and is glorified in the scripture that deals with it.[27]

(*Devatā-tantra*)

5. *Meditation*

The worshipper should engage in meditation, gradually concentrating his mind on all the parts of the body of his chosen deity, one after another, from the feet to the head. He can thus acquire such an intense state of concentration that during his undisturbed meditation the whole body of the chosen deity will appear to his mind's eye as an indivisible form. In this way the meditation of the deity in its formal aspect will gradually become profound and steady.[27]

(*Principles of Tantras*)

6. *The Tântric "Full Initiation" Ceremony, According to the Kaula School*

In the three ages[a] this rite was a great secret; men then used to perform it in all secrecy, and thus attained Liberation.

When the Kali age[b] prevails, the followers of Kula rite[c] should declare themselves as such, and, whether in the night or the day, should openly be initiated.

The Guru[c] should, the day before the initiation, worship Gaṇeśa[d] with offerings, according to his ability for the removal of all obstacles. Adding successively six long vowels to the Mūla *mantra,*[d] Nyāsa[e] on the six parts of the body should be performed, and after doing the three breath-exercises let Gaṇeśa[f] be meditated upon.

Meditate on Gaṇeśa as of the colour of vermilion, having three eyes, a large belly, holding in his lotus-hands the conch, the noose, the elephant-goad, and the sign of blessing. His great trunk is adorned with the jar of wine which it holds. On his forehead shines the young Moon. He has the head of the King of elephants; his cheeks are constantly bathed in wine. His body is adorned with the coils of the King of servants. He is dressed in red raiment, and his body is smeared with scented ointments.

Having thus meditated upon Gaṇeśa, he should be worshipped with mental offerings, and then the protective powers of the seat should be worshipped. At the end, the Lotus-seat itself should be worshipped.

Meditating on Gaṇeśa once again, he should be worshipped with offerings of the Five-Elements (wine, meat, fish, parched food, and woman). After, the worshipper should perform the preliminary ceremony, and then entertain the Kaulas versed in divine knowledge with the Five-Elements. The next day, having bathed and performed his ordinary daily duties, he should give away sesamum-seed and gold for the destruction of all sins from his birth. Then, having worshipped Brahmā, Viṣṇu, Śiva, and the nine Planets, as also the sixteen divine Mothers, he should make a mark like the lower half of an ellipse.

He should ask permission of the spiritual Preceptor; then make a solemn declaration for the removal of all obstacles and for the attainment of long life, prosperity, strength, and good health.

He should do honour to the *guru,* by presenting him with clothes and jewels, and invite him to perform the rite.

The *guru* should then make with earth an altar four fingers in height and measuring one and a half cubits either way in a beautiful room painted with red earth, etc., decorated with pictures, flags, fruits, and leaves, and strings of small bells.

The room should have a beautiful ceiling-cloth, lighted with lines of lamps fed with ghee to dispel all traces of darkness, and should be scented with burning camphor, incense-sticks, and incense, and ornamented with fans, fly-whisks, the tail feathers of the peacock, and mirrors, etc., and then he should with rice, powdered and coloured yellow, red, black, white, and dark blue draw the circle called *Sarvato-bhadra.*

Then each person should perform the rite preparatory to mental worship, according to his own ritual, and then, should purify the Five-Elements with the formula previously mentioned. After the Five-Elements have been purified, the jar, which must be either of gold or silver or copper or earth, should be placed on the circle. It should be washed with the

Weapon-formula and smeared with curd, and then a vermilion mark should be placed on it.

He should then recite three times the letters of the alphabet, and fill the jar with wine or water from some holy place, or with ordinary pure water, and then throw into the jar nine gems or a piece of gold.

The merciful *guru* should then place over the mouth of the jar a leafy branch of a Fig-tree, etc.

He should then place on the leafy branches a gold, silver, copper, or earthen platter with fruits and sundried rice. Then two pieces of cloth should be tied to the neck of the jar. When worshipping Śakti the cloth should be of a red colour, and in the worship of Śiva and Viṣṇu it should be white.

The jar should be put in its place, and after putting into it the Five-Elements the nine cups should be placed in their order.

After placing the cups, libations should be offered to the four *gurus* and the divine Mother, and the wise one should then worship the jar filled with nectar. Lights and incense should be waved and sacrifices made to all beings, and after worshipping the divinities of the sacred Seats he should perform the *Nyāsa*[e] on the six parts of the body. He should then do the three breath-exercises, and, meditating on the great Mother, invoke her, and thereafter worship her to the best of his ability. The *guru* should perform all the rites, and then honour the unmarried girls and worshippers of Śakti[g] by presenting them with flowers, sandal-paste, and clothes.

The *guru* should then make the disciple worship the divine Mother in the jar, and then, mentally repeating the formula "Klīṃ, hrīṃ, śrīṃ" over it, move the pure jar, with the following formula:

"Rise, O jar who art Brahman, thou art the divinity and grantest all success. May my disciple, being bathed with thy waters and leaves, be devoted to Brahman."

Having moved the jar in this manner, the *guru* should mercifully sprinkle the disciple seated with his face to the North with the formulas about to be spoken. . . .

With these twenty-one formulas the disciple should be sprinkled with water; and if he has obtained already the formula from the mouth of a non-initiated, the *guru* should make him hear it again.

The *guru* of the Kaula school should, having informed the worshippers of Śakti, call his disciple by his name and give a name ending with *Anandanātha*. Being thus initiated in the formula by the *guru,* the disciple should worship his divinity of election in the sacred diagram and then honour the *guru* by offering him the Five-Elements.

The disciple should also give as ritual presents cows, land, gold, clothes, drinks, and jewels to the *guru,* and then honour the Kaulas, who are the very embodiments of Śiva.

The Kaulas who have been *fully initiated* are pure of soul. All things are purified by their look, touch, and when smelt by them. All men should worship the Kaula holy man with devotion.[28]

(*Mahānirvana-tantra,* 10.109–199)

[a] The three past ages of humanity.
[b] The present (evil) age.
[c] Tantra according to the Kaula school.
[d] Basic sacred formula.
[e] Assignment of various parts of the body to tutelary deities.
[f] The god of wisdom and of obstacles.
[g] Divine female principle, personified energy.

7. *The Supreme Female Deity*

[The poet invokes the vision of Devī, the Supreme Female Deity, seated in her mansion in the isle of gems, on a couch composed of Śiva and the other gods. She ascends by the *kula* path to the thousand-petalled lotus, causing her "*kuṇḍalinī*" power to pierce the six circles of the universe. Then she returns by descent along the same path to her place in the "*kulakuṇḍa*" hollow, where she sleeps in the form of a serpent. Her mansion is the "*śrīcakra,*" the mystic diagram. Her beauty is beyond the power of poets to depict. She sits in the lotus above the six circles. The sight of her in the lotus brings supreme joy to those few mighty ones who gain it. Let the author but have this ecstatic vision and achieve identity with her.]

(8) In the midst of the Ocean of Nectar, where covered with groves of heavenly wishing trees is the Isle of Gems, in the mansion of wishing jewels with its grove of *nīpa* trees, on a couch composed of Śiva and the other gods, your seat a mattress which is Supreme Śiva —some few lucky ones worship you, a flood of consciousness and bliss.

(9) The earth in the *mūlādhāra,* the water in the *maṇipūra,* the fire situated in the *svādhiṣṭhāna,* the air in the heart, and the ether above it, the mind between the eyebrows —in short, having pierced the entire *kula* path, in the thousand-petalled lotus you sport in secret with your lord.[a]

(10) With streams of nectar flowing from between your feet sprinkling the universe, recreating through the power of reciting the sacred texts that produce the six circles, again you reach your own abode and into the form of a serpent in three and a half coils[b] you convert yourself and sleep in the *kulakuṇḍa* hollow.

(11) By reason of the four and the five triangles, which are pierced by the *bindu* and constitute the nine basic triangles, forty-three—along with the lotuses of eight and sixteen petals outside the triangles and the three circles outside the lotuses and the three lines outside the circles—angles of your dwelling place are evolved.[c]

(12) To equal your beauty, O daughter of the snowy mountain, master poets can scarcely succeed; the heavenly courtesans, when they have glimpsed it, through their longing to enjoy it pass in imagination to identify with the Mountain-dweller Śiva, who is hard to attain even by ascetic practices. . . .

(14) In earth fifty-six, fifty-two in water, in fire sixty-two, fifty-four in air, in ether seventy-two, and in mind sixty-four—these are the rays; above them in the thousand-petalled lotus is the pair of your lotus feet. . . .[d]

(21) Slender as a streak of lightning, composed of the essence of sun, moon, and fire, situated above the six lotuses, the manifestation of you in the forest of great lotuses, those with mind free of stain and illusion who view it, mighty ones, experience a flood of supreme joy.

(22) "Do you, O lady, extend to me, your slave, a compassionate glance!"—when one desiring to praise you utters the words "you, O lady,"[e] at that moment you grant him a state of identity with you, with your feet illuminated[f] by the crests of Viṣṇu, Brahmā, and Indra.[29]

[a] The cosmos evolves in six stages, which are described anthropomorphically as six circles in the cosmos conceived as Devī's body. Mūlādhāra, etc., are the names of the six circles. At the top of the universe, or anthropomorphically at the top of Devī's head, is the thousand-petaled lotus, in which the feminine and masculine principles coexist.

[b] In the cosmos conceived as Devī's body the feminine power exists as a sleeping serpent called *kuṇḍalinī* in the *kuṇḍa* hollow at the bottom of the six circles.

[c] Devī's diagram is called her mansion, and is described as consisting of triangles, and in the middle of these the *bindu* ("drop"), which seems to be the masculine element. Around the angles are two lotuses; outside these are three circles, and finally three squares.

[d] The above-mentioned six circles.

[e] Which also means, "May I be you."

[f] As in the evening waving of lights before a god's image.

XIII. Kālidāsa

Kālidāsa is the greatest name in the lyrical poetry of India. His works, which are probably to be placed in the fourth or fifth centuries, comprise many dramatical comedies (including the famous *Śakuntalā* and at least three works of the "lyrical epic" type. His verses narrate the life of the descendants of the hero Raghu (the *Raghuvaṃśa*), the meeting of the god Śiva and Pārvatī and the birth of their son Kumāra (the *Kumārasambhava*), a lyrical love-elegy (the "Cloud Messenger" or *Meghadūta*), and so on. Exalting alike the virtues of the saint or the hero, his works are rich in mythological allusions and in maxims; they represent the Brahmanic ideal in its perfection of harmony.

1. *Kumāra's Fight against the Demon Tāraka*

A fearful flock of evil birds,
ready for the joy of eating the army of demons,
flew over the host of the gods,
and clouded the sun.

A wind continually fluttered their umbrellas and banners,
and troubled their eyes with clouds of whirling dust,
so that the trembling horses and elephants
and the great chariots could not be seen.

Suddenly monstrous serpents, as black as powdered soot,
scattering poison from their upraised heads,
frightful in form,
appeared in the army's path.

The sun put on a ghastly robe
of great and terrible snakes, curling together,
as if to mark his joy
at the death of the enemy demon.

And before the very disc of the sun
jackals bayed harshly together,
as though eager fiercely to lap the blood
of the king of the foes of the gods, fallen in battle.

Lighting heaven from end to end,
with flames flashing all around,
with an awful crash, rending the heart with terror,
a thunderbolt fell from a cloudless sky.

The sky poured down torrents of red-hot ashes,
with which were mixed blood and human bones,
till the flaming ends of heaven were filled with smoke
and bore the dull hue of the neck of an ass.

Like the thundered threat of the angry death-god
a great crash broke the walls of the ears,
a shattering sound, tearing the tops of the mountains,
and wholly filling the belly of heaven.

The host of the foe was jostled together.
The great elephants stumbled, the horses fell,
and all the footmen clung together in fear,
as the earth trembled and the ocean rose to shake the mountains.

And, before the host of the foes of the gods,
dogs lifted their muzzles to gaze on the sun,
then, howling together with cries that rent the eardrums,
they wretchedly slunk away.[30]

(*Kumāra-sambhava,* 15.14)

2. *The Destruction of Kāma, the God of Love, by Śiva*

. . . But Kāma, seeing an opportunity for his arrow, like a moth eager to enter the mouth of the flame, in the very presence of Umā[a] fixing his aim on Hara[b] repeatedly fingered the bow-string.

Then Gaurī[c] presented to the ascetic mountain-dwelling god with a hand bright as copper a rosary of lotus-seeds from the Ganges, dried by the rays of the sun.

And the three-eyed god[d] made to receive it, through kindness towards his worshipper; and the flower-archer[e] laid to his bow the unfailing arrow called "Fascination."

But Hara,[b] his firmness somewhat disturbed, like the ocean when the moon begins to rise, kept his gaze fixed on Umā's[a] face, with lips like the *bimba*-fruit.[f]

And the daughter of the mountain,[a] betraying her emotion by her limbs like quivering young *kadamba*-shoots, stood with head bent, her face all the more lovely with her turned-away glance.

Then the three-eyed god, with an effort regaining command of the perturbation of his senses by reason of his power of self-control, cast his glance in all directions, desirous to see the cause of the disturbance of his mind.

He saw the mind-born god,[d] his clenched fist raised to the outer corner of his right eye, his shoulder bent, his left leg bent, his delicate bow drawn into a circle, ready to strike.

His anger increased by the attack on his austerity, his face terrible to look upon with its frowning brows, from his third eye of a sudden a blazing glittering flame came forth.

While the voices of the wind-gods passed across the sky—"Restrain, restrain your anger, Lord," the fire born from the eye of Bhava[b] reduced the god of love to a residue of ashes.

The swoon caused by the bitter shock, checking the operation of the senses, performed for Rati[g] almost a kindly service, and for a short while she knew not of the disaster which had befallen her husband.

Having swiftly shattered the obstacle to his asceticism, like the thunderbolt a forest-tree, he, the ascetic, the Lord of Creatures,[b] wishing to escape from the proximity of women, vanished along with his creatures.

And the daughter of the mountain,[a] thinking that her mighty father's desire and her own charming form were vain, her shame increased by the thought that her two friends had been present, desolate she went with difficulty towards her dwelling-place.

And as her eyes closed from fear of the violence of Rudra,[b] the Mountain on the instant took up his piteous daughter in his arms, and like the heavenly elephant bearing a lotus clinging to his tusks, he pressed onwards, his limbs large with haste.[31]

(*Ibid.*, 3.64–76)

[a] God Śiva's wife and Himavant's (i.e., Himalaya's) daughter.
[b] Another name for Śiva.
[c] Another name for Umā.
[d] Kāma.
[e] Kāma.
[f] A red fruit.
[g] Kāma's wife, voluptuousness personified.

XIV. Bhartṛhari

To Bhartṛhari, an author of the seventh century, we owe stanzas on love, worldly wisdom and renunciation. These stanzas are collected in three "centuries" and form an epitome of rare formal perfection. They exemplify the moral values at the basis of Hinduism.

Scattered Stanzas

Your hair self-denying, your eyes understanding the whole of scripture,
your mouth full of groups of naturally-pure *brāhmans,*
your breasts lovely from the presence of emancipated souls,
slim girl, your body, though free from passion, disturbs me.[a]

What is the use of many idle speeches!
Only two things are worth a man's attention—
the youth of full-breasted women, prone to fresh pleasures,
and the forest.

When I was ignorant in the dark night of passion
I thought the world completely made of women,

but how my eyes are cleansed with the salve of wisdom,
and my clear vision sees only God in everything.

Oh Earth, my mother, Air, my father, Oh Fire, my friend,
Water, my kinsman, Space, my brother,
here do I bow before you with folded hands!
With your aid I have done good deeds and found clear knowledge,
and, glorious, with all delusion past, I merge in highest godhead.[32]

[a] The obvious meaning being:
Your hair well combed, your eyes reaching to your ears,
your mouth filled with ranks of teeth that are white by nature,
your breasts charmingly adorned with a necklace of pearls,
slim girl, your body, though at rest, disturbs me.

Thou hear'st that from thy neighbour's stores
Some goods by theft have vanished; so,
That none of thine by stealth may go,
Thou sett'st a watch, and barr'st thy doors.
'Tis well: but know'st thou never fear
When thou dost learn that every day
Stern death from many a dwelling near
A helpless victim tears away?
Deluded mortals, warning take,
From such insensate slumber wake!

Hark here the sound of lute so sweet,
And there the voice of wailing loud;
Here scholars grave in conclave meet,
There howls the brawling drunkard-crowd;
Here charming maidens full of glee,
There tottering, withered dames, we see.
Such light. Such shade. I cannot tell
If here we live in heaven or hell.[33]

Blinded by self-conceit and knowing nothing,
Like elephant infatuate with passion,
I thought within myself, I all things knew;
But when by slow degrees I somewhat learnt,
By aid of wise preceptors, my conceit,
Like some disease, passed off; and now I live
In the plain sense of what a fool I am.[34]

(2.8)

The attribute most noble of the hand
Is readiness in giving; of the head,
Bending before a teacher; of the mouth,
Veracious speaking; of a victor's arms,
Undaunted valour; of the inner heart,
Pureness the most unsullied; of the ears,
Delight in hearing and receiving truth—
These are adornments of high-minded men
Better than all the majesty of Empire.[34]

(2.55)

Better be thrown from some high peak,
Or dashed to pieces, falling upon rocks;
Better insert the hand between the fangs
Of an envenomed serpent; better fall
Into a fiery furnace, than destroy
The character by stains of infamy.[34]

(2.77)

Now for a little while a child, and now
An amorous youth; then for a season turned
Into the wealthy householder; then stripped
Of all his riches, with decrepit limbs
And wrinkled frame, man creeps towards the end
Of life's erratic course; and, like an actor,
Passes behind Death's curtain out of view.[34]

(3.51)

XV. Bhavabhuti

We owe to this eighth-century author three famous dramas, of which the two better known are a dramatized story of the later days of the hero Rāma (the *Uttararāma-carita*) and a love story interspersed with tragic scenes (the *Mālatīmādhava*). The excerpt below is a scene from the latter which demonstrates the preparation for a human sacrifice in honour of Cāmuṇḍā, one of the innumerable designations of the great Goddess.

A Human Sacrifice to Cāmuṇḍā, the Consort of God Śiva

Now wake the terrors of the place, beset
With crowding and malignant fiends; the flames
From funeral pyres scarce lend their sullen light
Clogged with their fleshy prey to dissipate
The fearful gloom that hems them in. Pale ghosts
Spirit with foul goblins, and their dissonant mirth
In shrill respondent shrieks is echoed round.

[Entry of the priestess]

Glory to Śaktināth,[a] upon whose steps,
The mighty goddesses attend, whom seek
Successfully alone the firm of thought.
He crowns the lofty aims of those who know
And hold his form, as the pervading spirit,
That, one with their own essence, makes his seat
The heart, the lotus centre of the sphere
Sixfold by ten nerves circled. Such am I.
Freed from all perishable bonds, I view
The eternal soul embodied as the God,

Forced by my spells to tread the mystic labyrinth,
And rise in splendour throned upon my heart.
Hence through the many channelled veins I draw
The grosser elements of this mortal body,
And soar unwearied through the air, dividing
The water-shedding clouds. Upon my flight,
Horrific honours wait;—the hollow skulls,
That low descending from my neck depend,
Emit fierce music as they clash together,
Or strike the trembling plates that gird my loins!

[Mādhava, trying to save Mālatī, his beloved, promised as a victim, shakes off the demon hosts]

Race dastardly as hideous. All is plunged
In utter gloom. The rivers flows before me,
The boundary of the funeral ground that winds
Through mouldering bones its interrupted way.
Wild raves the torrent as it rushes past,
And rends its crumbling banks, the wailing owl
Hoots through its skirting groves, and to the sounds
The loud, long moaning jackal yells reply.

[Within the temple the human-sacrificing priest dances his Tântric dance]

Hail, hail! Cāmuṇḍā, mighty goddess, hail!
I glorify thy sport, when in the dance
That fills the court of Śiva with delight,
Thy foot descending spurns the earthly globe.
The elephant hide that robes thee, to thy steps
Swings to and fro: the whirling talons rend
The crescent on thy brow; from the torn orb
The trickling nectar falls, and every skull
That gems thy necklace laughs with horrid life.[35]

[a] Śiva.

XVI. Rāmānuja

Born in the region of Madras in the eleventh century, Rāmānuja instituted a form of *Vedānta* based on the notion of the "qualified *brāhman,*" that is a personal god endowed with attributes which comprehend souls and things. As a consequence, according to him, religious practice comprises a form of *bhakti*, or "devotion," which has in part an intellectual tendency. He introduced in his work the idea of *prapatti*, or "abandon" (to the divine will).

The thought of Rāmānuja is adopted by the sect of the Śrīvaiṣṇavas who themselves depend partly on the theoretical texts of Viṣṇuism, called *Saṃhitās*, and partly on the movement of the Āḷvārs.

How God Is Regarded by the Ignorant and by the Wise

Urged upon this compassion for mankind, God has assumed a human body so that he might be the refuge of all men; but they do not know him as He is. They consider him to be a man like they are, and they are ignorant of God's supreme state of being which is a boundless receptacle of compassion, generosity, goodness, love, etc., and is characterized by its human shape. So for the mere reason that God is their refuge in human shape, they consider him to be of the same class as other human beings and so are mistaken about him. They have assumed the bewildering natures of *rākṣasas* and *asuras*[a] which puts an end to God's supreme compassion in his humanity; their aspirations and enterprises remain fruitless, their knowledge of all God's creatures and of God himself is erroneous, and they have list all positive knowledge of anything because they regard God as a man.

Those, however, whose good *karman*[b] enables them to take refuge in God and who, released from the bondage of evil, assume a divine nature, know God to be the origin of all beings, the eternal Lord whose proper form, name and actions are beyond thought and speech and who has descended into human shape to rescue the *sādhus*,[c] and they worship God with all their minds focused on him alone. Because of their extreme love of God their minds, *ātmans*[d] and external organs lack all support no sooner than they cease to worship him by *bhakti*[e] or to praise him or to exert themselves for his sake; therefore they meditate on the names which denote God's special qualities. In an ecstasy of joy they glorify him by crying out his names Nārāyana, Kṛṣṇa, Vāsudeva, etc., and resolutely exert themselves to act for the glory of God, by worship and means of worship, such as the building of temples, gardens and groves, and they prostrate themselves indifferent to dust, mud and gravel with the eight members of the body desirous of everlasting union with God.

Other high-minded believers worship God by paying homage to him not only in the above way but also by performing the sacrifice called *jnana*.[f] What does that mean? They worship God as the One underlying the individual plurality of things. This means that they worship God with the certain knowledge that God is one and that his body is constituted by the manifold creation of gods, men, animals and immovables, because at the time when his body consisted of infinitesimally subtle spiritual and non-spiritual substances incapable of individual distinctness by name-and-form, God has decided on this volition: By my body constituted by gross spiritual and non-spiritual mass which exists in a plurality of individual forms distinguishable by name-and-form. So God's body is the universe, God is the sacrifice, the libation and oblation offered to nourish the deceased ancestors, etc. He is father, mother, grandfather and establisher of the world consisting of mobile and immobile creatures. He is the means of purification, the core of the Vedas, the Veda itself. He is the end to be attained, the supporter, the ruler, the immediate witness, the residence, the spiritual resort, the well-meaning friend. He is the place of origination and annihilation of whatever wherever. He is all that can be begotten or destroyed. He is the imperishable cause of all that. God heats in the form of fire, the sun, etc., at the beginning of summer; then again he stops the rains and pours out the rains. He is both that through which one lives and that through which one dies. He is the present, the past and the future. Those who through their knowledge of this essential unity of God realize that the whole world is a modification of God because God's body is constituted by the names-and-forms of a plurality of individual beings and who worship God as such, those are the true *mahātmans*.[g]

Those people, on the other hand, who are firmly fixed on the Vedas and not on the *Vedānta*,[h] who drink the *soma* beverage which is proper to the worship of mere divinities like Indra as prescribed by the Vedas, who are only purified from evil incompatible with the attainment of heaven, and who aspiring to heaven sacrifice to God as though he himself were the divinities because they do not know who God really is, those people will attain the world of Indra which is free from unhappiness and enjoy divine pleasures. But when the good *karman*[b] which led them to heaven is consumed, they will return to the world of mortals. Because they lack the knowledge taught by the *Vedānta*[h] they will return to *saṃsāra*[i] after having enjoyed the immaterial and transient pleasures of heaven.

The *mahātmans*,[g] however, will not return, for their only end in life is the meditation on God, because without it they are unable to sustain their *ātmans*.[d] They worship God in all his glory while aspiring to constant union with him, and God will lead them to *yoga* or attainment of God and to *kṣema* or no return.[j]

The ignorant, however, are devoted to mere divinities and so rely on the Vedas alone and faithfully sacrifice to these divinities. But while doing so they actually sacrifice to God himself, for everything constitutes God's body and as God is the self of everyone and everything, he may be called by the names of these divinities. But the ignorant perform their sacrifices without connecting them with the words of the *Vedānta.* The entire *Vedānta* lays down the doctrine that the divinities are to be worshipped in so far as they constitute the body of the Supreme Person, but that it actually is the Supreme Person himself who is the one to be worshipped, because he is their self. When performing their sacrifices the four *hotṛs*[k] will find the fulfilment of their desires via the divinities—who constitute God's body—in God who is the inner ruler of these divinities; or, in other words, when they know that by their acts they pay homage to God himself and then perform these acts—serving to reconcile the divinities—they will find in God the perfect fulfilment of their aspirations. The ignorant, however, do not know this, so their reward is but a small one and it is in their nature to fall back to *saṃsāra.*[j][36]

(*Gīta-bhasya,* 2)

[a] Two classes of demons.
[b] Human act and its results.
[c] Saints.
[d] Self.
[e] Emotional devotion to God.
[f] Knowledge.
[g] Literally, "great souls."
[h] The last and speculative part of the Vedas.
[i] Literally, "safety" (from *saṃsāra*).
[j] Return to earth after death; transmigration.
[k] Vedic officiating priests.

XVII. The *Gīta-govinda*

The *Song of Govinda* (Kṛṣṇa as a cowherd god) is the work of Jayadeva (Bengal, end of twelfth century). It describes the love of Kṛṣṇa and Rādhā, the nostalgia of the god from whom Rādhā is kept apart by rancor, the suffering of Rādhā, and their reconciliation. This pastoral, in which a mystical tone is mingled with that of lyric love, appears as a sort of a booklet consisting of a suite of cantilenas terminated by refrains.

1. *Kṛṣṇa's Longing When Separated from Rādhā*

Here I am dwelling. Go now to Rādhā,
console her with my message, and bring her to me.
Thus the foe of Madhu[a] commissioned her friend,
who went in person, and spoke to Rādhā thus:

When the breeze blows from the Southern Mountains,
and brings the Love-god with it,
when masses of flowers burst forth
to rend the hearts of parted lovers,
he is grieved at separation from you, decked with his forest garland.

Even the cool-rayed moon inflames him,
he is as if dead.
Struck by the arrows of love
he complains most wretchedly.
He is grieved. . . .

When the swarming bees are murmuring
he closes fast his ears.
His heart is clenched by parting,
he spends his nights in fever.
He is grieved. . . .

He dwells in the depths of the forest,
he has left his lovely home.
He tosses in sleep on the earth
and much he murmurs your name.
He is grieved. . . .

When the poet Jayadeva sings,
through this pious description

of the deeds of the parted lover,
may Hari arise in hearts full of zeal.
He is grieved. . . .[37]

[a] Kṛṣṇa himself.

2. *Rādhā's Grief at Separation Described to Kṛṣṇa*

She secretly sees you everywhere, drinking the sweet honey of her lips. Lord Hari,[a] Rādhā pines in the lovers' bower.

As she hastens in her eagerness to go to meet you, she moves a few steps, and falls in a swoon. Lord Hari, Rādhā pines in the lovers' bower.

Wearing a bracelet made from pure white lotus-stalks and young shoots, she lives on here only by reason of your skill in love. Lord Hari, Rādhā pines in the lovers' bower.

Observing time and again the playful beauty of her ornaments, she pretends that she herself is the Enemy of Madhu.[b] Lord Hari, Rādhā pines in the lovers' bower.

"Why does Hari not come quickly to the place of assignation?" she says to her companion time and time again. Lord Hari, Rādhā pines in the lovers' bower.

She embraces and kisses the great darkness, like to a raincloud, thinking, "Hari has come." Lord Hari, Rādhā pines in the lovers' bower.

While you delay, modesty, goes from her, and she bewails and weeps, bedecked for her lover. Lord Hari, Rādhā pines in the lovers' bower.

May this utterance of the poet Jayadeva bestow great happiness on those who appreciate poetry. Lord Hari, Rādhā pines in the lovers' bower.[38]

(Song 12)

[a] Viṣṇu.
[b] Kṛṣṇa himself.

XVIII. The *Sarva-darśana-saṃgraha* of Mādhava

This treatise is a résumé of the principal systems of Indian philosophy. It dates from the fourteenth century. We include it here since the first system described in it is that of the Cārvakas, or Materialists. The preponderance of religious texts in India should not let us forget that there have been movements of agnostics, sceptics and atheists whose literature is almost entirely lost. The part they played should not be ignored when an attempt is made to trace the aspects and limits of the religious character of India.

Indian Atheism

There is no heaven, no final liberation, nor any soul in another world,
Nor do the actions of the four castes, orders, etc., produce any real effect.
The Agnihotra,[a] the three Vedas, the ascetic's three staves, and smearing one's self with ashes,
Were made by Nature as the livelihood of those destitute of knowledge and manliness.
If a beast slain in the Jyotiṣṭoma rite[b] will itself go to heaven,
Why then does not the sacrificer forthwith offer his own father?
If the Śrāddha[c] produces gratification to beings who are dead,
Then here, too, in the case of travellers when they start, it is needless to give provisions for the journey.
If beings in heaven are gratified by our offering the Śrāddha here,
Then why not give the food down below to those who are standing on the housetop?

While life remains let a man live happily, let him feed on ghee even though he runs in debt;
When once the body becomes ashes, how can it ever return again?
If he who departs from the body goes to another world,
How is it that he comes not back again, restless for love of his kindred?
Hence it is only as a means of livelihood that Brahmins have established here
All these ceremonies for the dead,—there is no other fruit anywhere.
The three authors of the Vedas were buffoons, knaves, and demons.
All the well-known formulae of the paṇḍits, *jarpharī, turpharī,* etc.[d]
And all the obscene rites for the queen commanded in the Aśvamedha,[e]
These were invented by buffoons, and so all the various kinds of presents to the priests,
While the eating of flesh was similarly commanded by night-prowling demons.[39]

[a] The daily fire oblation.
[b] A complicated Vedic ceremony.
[c] A commemorative rite in honor of the dead.
[d] Obscure words of the Ṛg-veda.
[e] The horse sacrifice.

XIX. The *Adhyātma-Rāmāyaṇa*

An edifying poem in 4,200 double verses, which combines a Tântric purpose with a moral borrowed from the *Rāmāyaṇa*. This is a "*Rāmāyaṇa* on the plane of the *ātman*." Herein is to be seen a dialogue between Śiva and the Goddess on the divine character of Rāmā and Sītā. The work must date from the fifteenth century.

The *Karman*

None can ever be the cause of fortune or misfortune of another. The *karman* which we have ourselves accumulated in the past, that alone is the cause of fortune and misfortune. To attribute one's fortune and misfortune to another is an error, as it is a vain pride to think: "It is I who am the author of this," for all beings are bound by the chain of their *karman.* If man fancies to himself that some beings are his friends, others his enemies or are indifferent to him, it is according to the *karman* that he has worked out himself. It is necessary, therefore, that man should bear with one mind his fortune and misfortune, which are only fruits of his own actions. He should say unto himself: "I desire neither to obtain enjoyments nor to be deprived of them; whether I acquire them or not, it is just the same"; and thus he should not be a slave. In whatever situation, whatever time, and for whatever reasons, man accomplishes an action, good or bad, he must submit to its consequences accordingly.

It is therefore in vain that he rejoices or is aggrieved of a happy or an unhappy event, because the decrees of Destiny are inevitable even for demons and gods. Man can never escape pleasure or pain, because his body, which is a product of his good or bad actions, is by nature transient. After pleasure pain, after pain pleasure: creatures cannot escape these two, as they cannot the succession of day and night. They are intimately associated as water and mud. It is, therefore, that Sages knowing that all is but illusion, remain steadfast and neither are aggrieved nor joyous for events unhappy and happy.[40]

(2.6, 14–16)

B. Non-Sanskritic Sources

I. Appar

The poet Appar belongs to that vast flowering of the Shaivite religious character which marks Tamil literature from the seventh century. He is perhaps the most ardent of the group of Nāyanārs or "Shaivite saints" who demand an exclusive faith in Śiva and set aside all religious practices and all texts.

1. *Confession of Sin*

Evil, all evil, my race, evil my qualities all,
Great am I only in sin, evil is even my good.
Evil my innermost self, foolish, avoiding the pure,
Beast am I not, yet the ways of the beast I can never
forsake.
I can exhort with strong words, telling men what
they should hate,
Yet can I never give gifts, only to beg them I know.
Ah! wretched man that I am, whereunto came I to
birth?[41]

2. *Presence of God*

No man holds sway o'er us,
Nor death nor hell fear we;
No tremblings, griefs of mind,
No pains nor cringings see.
Joy, day by day, unchanged
Is ours, for we are His,

His ever, who doth reign,
Our Śankara,[a] in bliss.
Here to His feet we've come,
Feet as plucked flow'rets fair;
See how His ears divine
Ring and white conch-shell wear.[41]

[a] Śiva.

He is ever hard to find, but He lives in the thought of the good;
He is innermost secret of Scripture, inscrutable, unknowable;
He is honey and milk and the shining light. He is the king of the Devas,
Immanent in Viṣṇu, in Brahmā, in flame and in wind,
Yet in the mighty sounding sea and in the mountains.
He is the great One who chooses Perumpattapuliyûr[a] for His own.
If there be days when my tongue is dumb and speaks not of Him,
Let no such days be counted in the record of my life.[41]

[a] Śiva's paradise.

II. Māṇikka Vāçagar

Belonging to the end of the seventh century, this poet, Ashowas, chief minister of a Pāṇḍya king, is the most classical mystic of South India. His odes are used in the Shaivite liturgy of the Tamil region. They express a militant monotheism which insists on devoted love and on divine Grace.

1. *Life's Consuming*

Myself I cannot understand, nor what is day nor night;
He who both word and thought transcends has reft my senses quite,
He who for bull has Viṣṇu, and in Perundurai[a] dwells,
O Light supreme, in Brahmana guise has cast on me strange spells.

I ask not fame, wealth, earth or heav'n. No birth, no death for me.
None will I touch who love not Śiva. Now 'tis mine to see
Abiding Perundurai, wear the King's foot as my crown;
Never will I leave this His shrine, nor let Him leave His own.

Art Thou like honey on the branch too high for me to climb?
Or art Thou nectar ocean-churned? O Hara,[b] King sublime,
In Perundurai, circled with moist fields, I can see Thee
With form ash-smeared, the spotless. Can I bear my ecstasy?

Many in this great earth who live do penance; I alone
Bearing this frame of flesh, a barren jungle-tree have grown.
Dweller in Perundurai old where blooms the kondai tree,
May I the sinner cry "Wilt Thou not grant Thyself to me?"

[a] Śiva's paradise.
[b] Śiva.

2. *Pious Fear*

I fear not serpents lurking smooth;
I fear no liars' feignèd truth;
But when I see fools venturing
E'en to the foot of Him our king,
Our three-eyed Lord with matted hair,
Of His great godhead unaware,
Fools thinking other gods can be,
Terror such sight inspires in me.

3. *Naught but Thy Love*

I ask not kin, nor name, nor place,
Nor learnèd men's society.
Men's lore for me no value has;
Kuttâlam's lord, I come to Thee.
Wilt thou one boon on me bestow,
A heart to melt in longing sweet,
As yearns o'er new-born calf the cow,
In yearning for Thy sacred feet?

4. *Longing for Union*

I had no virtue, penance, knowledge, self-control. A doll to turn
At others' will I danced, whirled, fell. But me He filled in every limb
With love's mad longing, and that I might climb there whence is no return,
He shewed His beauty, made me His. Ah me, when shall I go to Him?[42]

III. The Āḷvārs

Also from the Tamil region are a dozen Vaiṣṇavite Āḷvārs who parallel the Shaivite Nāyanārs. The most well known among them was Nammāḷvār (of indefinite date) who was the author of *Tiruviruttam,* or "Sacred Words," which laud Viṣṇu and his *avatāras,* notably Kṛṣṇa, the cowherd god, and the cowherdess. This work consists of a suite of odes quite learned in character.

Longing for Kṛṣṇa

[Invocation: the Āḷvār prays to be delivered from rebirth]

Be gracious, Lord of all the heavenly ones,
Born in all births to save all lives, and hear
Thy servant's plea. Grant, not again may I
Such nature win as this—my body foul,
Wisdom unsound, and character defiled.

[The maid speaks, seeing the state of her mistress, unable to endure separation from her lord, who has left her. Here the maid stands for the Āḷvār's disciples, the mistress for the Āḷvār, the lord for Viṣṇu]

Long may she love, this girl with luring looks,
Who loves the feet that heavenly ones adore,
The feet of Kaṇṇan,[a] dark as rainy clouds:
Her red eyes all abrim with tears of grief,
Like darting Kayal fish in a deep pool.

[The mistress to her maid]

Will't stay or come again, my lonely heart
Which has pursued the bird[b] flame-angry, driven
By the lord of tulasī,[c] arm'd with fatal wheel,
Whom gods adore!—The piping cowherds' girl,[d]
Bhūdevī, Śrī,[e] his shadows, it perceives!

[Plaint of the mistress]

Wind that art tulasī-poisoned, blowing thoughts
Of him who drain'd the traitress demon's breast,[f]
Oh, shame to come and with trembling me,—
Me, whom his bird ere now of her one heart
Has reft! No heart for tulasī remains.

[The pity of the maid on seeing her mistress' loss of color through grief]

Hot in this village now doth blow the breeze
Whose nature coolness is. Hath he, this once,
The rain-cloud hued, his sceptre turned aside
To steal the love-glow from my lady, lorn
For tulasī, with wide eyes raining tears?

[The mistress is troubled at the coming of the rainy season, which should have brought her lord back to her]

Is this the sky in which the strong dark bulls[g]
Pawing the ground till Earth shakes, sweat and fight?
Is this the cool fair time that takes the form
Of Viṣṇu, and sounds his harshness who
Is gone? Sinful, I know not what I see.

[The lord—here the Āḷvār's devotees—speaks of the difficulty of parting from his mistress]

Ah, who can leave her, like a creeper hung
With glorious flowers, like unto Viṣṇu's heaven?
Are these but eyes? Nay, lotus, lilies red,
Wide petals, lined in black, and all abrim
With pearls of white—wide, like a shy deer's eyes.

[The words of the lord on seeing his mistress' eyes fill with tears]

Oh rare the vision of today! Thou maid
That givest bliss like Kaṇṇan's heaven, I say
"He that seeks wealth must needs go far"—and lo!
Thy fish-like eyes, large as a hand, with pearls
Ashine, and gold, a ransom for the world!

[Lamentation of the mistress]

Love's glow is paling, and instead, a dark
And sickly yellow spreading;—and the night
Becomes an age! This is the matchless wealth
My good heart gave me when it yearned and sought
Keen discus-wielding Kaṇṇan's tulasī cool![43]

(*Tiruvittam*, 1–12)

[a] Kṛṣṇa.
[b] Garuḍa, the vehicle of Viṣṇu.
[c] The holy basil, a plant dedicated to Viṣṇu.
[d] Rādhā, Kṛṣṇa's consort.
[e] Two other consorts of Viṣṇu.
[f] Kṛṣṇa's infant sucked the life out of the demon.
[g] The rain clouds.

IV. The *Śivañānabôdham*

This didactic treatise is attributed to Meykaṇḍadevar and is composed in Tamil. It is a commentary on twelve Sanskrit *sūtras* called the *Śaivasiddhānta* which serve as a basic text of the Shaivite school of south India. The work dates from the thirteenth century. We reproduce below the translation of these *sūtras*.

The True Śivaite Doctrine

Because the world exists in forms male, female, and neuter, it is seen as an effect; therefore there must be an Agent. He after having dissolved it creates it; therefore Hara[a] is Lord.

Although the Agent is other than souls, He is not other by reason of pervasion. Through the Power which is inseparably associated with Him, He causes transmigration for human beings in conformity with their deeds.

There exists a subtle essence in the body; because there is something which is "not this or that"; because of the excess of "mine-ness"; because of the awakening and the stopping of the eye;[b] because of the absence of enjoyment of the senses in sleep; because there is an agent of perception in perception.

Although the soul is different from the inner organ, it is associated with it like a king with his counsellors, and must exist in the five states, with the function of its own seeing obstructed by impurity.

The eyes perceive the objects of human sense, not of themselves but by the soul. The soul knows by the help of Śambhu.[a] If one should say Śiva is then subject to change, the answer would be nay, He draws him as magnet the iron.

If He were the imperceptible, He would be non-existent. If He were the perceptible, He would be insentient matter. Therefore the wise understand that the form of Śambhu is knowable because it is different from this.

In the presence of the Conscious, there is no Non-conscious. Yet they are twain, but do not know each other. The knower of the world and of Śiva is the knower's soul, which is different from both.

When the blest soul, after having dwelt together with the hunters, the senses, is instructed by a guru,[c] "Thou knowest not thyself," then after having given up these senses, being not other than Śiva, he reaches His feet.

Through spiritual vision having seen the Lord[a] in the soul, and having abandoned the mirage of the senses' activity and having grasped the shadow of Śiva's feet, the sage should meditate upon the Five Letters.

So the perfected one who has attained union with Śiva, being dependent upon Him, has His activity; and being untouched by impurity and Māyā[c] and the like, has His experience.

The soul makes the eyes see; and Śiva is the maker of the

soul's seeing. Therefore one should pay great devotion to Him who is the helper of the soul.

For the sake of release, having approached the righteous, one should offer devotion to their habit and to the dwelling-place of Śiva; and thus understand the settled doctrines of Śaivism in the *Śivañānabôdham*.[44]

[a] Śiva.
[b] Used for all the senses.
[c] Cosmic illusion, or nescience.

V. Lallā

Lallā, the prophetess of Kaśmir who lived in the fourteenth century, taught a method of Yoga which is connected with Kaśmirian Shaivism and has "*advaita*" *Vedānta* as a basis. Her novel contribution to the religious tonality of India lies not so much in that she knew and assimilated the sûfi doctrines as that, with the elaborate and often very esoteric symbols which she adopted, she preserved or discovered a most pure and profound mystical sentiment.

A Spiritual Experience

[Lallā commences by relating her own spiritual experience. She had wandered far and wide in search of the truth, but all in vain. Then suddenly she found it in her own soul. There she found her own self, which became to her the equivalent of a spiritual preceptor and she learned that it and the Supreme Self (Śiva) were one]

Passionate, with longing in mine eyes,
  Searching wide, and seeking nights and days,
Lo! I behold the Truthful One, the Wise,
  Here in mine own House to fill my gaze.

That was the day of my lucky star.
  Breathless, I held him my Guide to be.
So my Lamp of Knowledge blazed afar,
  Fanned by slow breath from the throat of me.

Then, my bright Soul to my Self revealed,
  Winnowed I abroad my inner Light;
And with darkness all around me sealed
  Did I garner Truth and hold him tight.

[Being a professed *yoginī,* her mysticism and transcendentalism is filled with the terms of the *Yoga* system and with references thereto]

When the Body-exercise is done
  And the last effort of Thought employed,
Then nor the End nor the Bourne is won.
  Brahman, this is Doctrine unalloyed.

When by Discipline repeated oft
  All the Wide is lifted to the Void,
Universe and Ether merge aloft.
  Brahman, this is Doctrine unalloyed.

When the Void within itself is solved
  And Ethereality destroyed,
Only is Well-being unresolved.
  Brahman, this is Doctrine unalloyed.

Where is the Weal, there no thought of mind,
  Action nor inaction may intrude;
Vows of silence entry fail to find,
  Nor avails the mystic attitude.

There nor even Śiva reigns supreme,
  Nor his wedded Energy hath sway.
Only is the Somewhat, like a dream,
  There pursuing an elusive way.

[Lallā is passionately devoted to the doctrine of the oneness of the individual self with the Supreme Self]

Lord, myself not always have I known;
  Nay, nor any other self than mine.
Care for this vile body have I shown,
  Mortified by me to make me Thine.

Lord, that I am Thou I did not know,
  Nor that Thou art I, that One be Twain.
"Who am I?" is Doubt of doubts, and so
  "Who art Thou?" shall lead to birth again.

Śiva or Keśava,[a] Lotus-Lord[b] or Jin:[c]
  These be Names. Yet takes Thou from me
All the ill that is my World within;
  He be Thou, or he, or he, or he.

[It is not works, but esoteric knowledge which will bring the soul Release or Salvation]

Lady,[d] rise and offer to the Name,
  Bearing in thy hand the flesh and wine.
Such shall never bring thee loss and shame,
  Be it of no custom that is thine.

This they know for Knowledge that have found—
  Be the loud Cry from His Place but heard—
Unity betwixt the Lord and Sound,
  Just as Sound hath unison with Word.

Feed thy fatted rams, thou worldly one,
 Take them grain and dainties, and then slay.
Give thy thoughts that reek with "said and done"
 Last-fruits of Knowledge, and cast away.

Then shalt see with Spirit-eyes the Place
 Where the dwelling of the Lord shall be:
Then shall pass thy terrors of disgrace:
 Then shall Custom lose her hold on thee.

"Think not on the things that are without:
 Fix upon thy inner Self thy Thought:
So shalt thou be freed from let or doubt":—
 Precepts these that my Preceptor taught.

Dance then, Lallā, clothed but by the air:
 Sing then, Lallā, clad but in the sky.
Air and sky: what garment is more fair?
 "Cloth," said Custom—Doth that sanctify?[45]

[a] Viṣṇu.
[b] God Brahmā.
[c] The Saviour of the Jains or of the Buddhists.
[d] = *Kuṇḍalinī*, the Power of the Spirit, the creative force of the phenomenal universe, resident in every human being's body.

VI. Nāmdev and Tukārām

Nāmdev, Maharashtrian poet, whom tradition places between the thirteenth and fourteenth centuries A.D., was heir to the founder of religious poetry that was Jñāneśvarai's. He was a representative of *bhakti* and a fervent follower of Viṣṇu.

Tukārām (1607–1649) was the greatest Maharashtrian poet. He was the author of about a thousand hymns called the *abhangs*. These hymns mark the culminating point of *bhakti*, a kind of worship free from all sectarian affiliations, from all ritual or learned influences. The *abhangs* are sung even today in the humblest of households in the Maharashtrian region of India.

The first selection below is by Nāmdev; the others, by Tukārām.

1. *The Reign of Peace*

Now all my days with joy I'll fill
Full to the brim,
With all my heart to Viṭṭhal[a] cling
And only him.

He will sweep utterly away
All dole and care;
And all in sunder shall I rend
Illusion's snare.

O altogether dear is he
And he alone,
For all my burden he will take
To be his own.

Lo, all the sorrow of the world
Will straightway cease,
And all unending now shall be
The reign of peace.

For all the bondage he will break
Of worldly care,
And all in sunder will he rend
Illusion's snare.

From all my foolish fancies now
Let me be free,
In Viṭṭhal, Viṭṭhal only is
Tranquillity.[46]

[a] Viṣṇu.

2. *Waiting*

With head on hand before my door,
  I sit and wait in vain.
Along the road to Paṇḍharī[a]
  My heart and eyes I strain.

When shall I look upon my Lord?
  When shall I see him come?
Of all the passing days and hours
  I count the heavy sum.

With watching long my eyelids throb,
  My limbs with sore distress,
But my impatient heart forgets
  My body's weariness.

Sleep is no longer sweet to me;
  I care not for my bed;
Forgotten are my house and home,
  All thirst and hunger fled.

Says Tukâ,[b] Blest shall be the day,—
  Ah, soon may it betide!—
When one shall come from Paṇḍharī
  To summon back the bride.[46]

[a] Or Paṇḍharpūr, seat of a celebrated temple to Viṣṇu.
[b] Tukārām himself.

3. *Keep Me from Vanity*

Keep me from vanity
  Keep me from pride,
For sure I perish if
  I quit thy side.

From this deceiving world
  How hard to flee!

Ah, thou, Vaikuṇṭha's[a] Lord,
  Deliver me!

If once thy gracious face
  I look upon,
The world's enticement then
  Is past and gone.[46]

[a] Viṣṇu's paradise.

4. *The Only Refuge*

I am a mass of sin;
  Thou art all purity;
Yet thou must take me as I am
  And bear my load for me.

Me Death has all consumed;
  In thee all power abides.
All else forsaking, at thy feet
  Thy servant Tukâ hides.[46]

5. *I Cannot Understand: I Love*

Thy greatness none can comprehend;
  All dumb the Vedas are.
Forspent the powers of mortal mind;
  They cannot climb so far.
How can I compass him whose light
  Illumes both sun and star?

The serpent of a thousand tongues[a]
  Cannot tell all thy praise;
Then how, poor I? Thy children we,
  Mother of loving ways!
Within the shadow of thy grace,
  Ah, hide me, Tukâ says.

[a] Śeṣa, the world-upholding snake.

6. *I Am Poor and Needy*

No deeds I've done nor thoughts I've
 thought;
Save as thy servant, I am nought.

Guard me, O God, and O, control
The tumult of my restless soul.

Ah, do not, do not cast on me
The guilt of mine iniquity.

My countless sins, I, Tukâ, say,
Upon thy loving heart I lay.[46]

VII. Kabīr

The work of Kabīr (1440–1518) is in vulgar Hindī and was transmitted orally. It consists of "words" in the form of short poems which ordinarily terminate in couplets. His doctrine is basically Hinduistic, but it was subject to Islamic influences.

Kabīr denies that religions, no matter what they be, permit an understanding of the mystery of God. He mentions that a mystical experience is necessary for understanding and that the instrument for mysticism is interiorized Yoga of the ascetic type. We reproduce in No. 3 a passage in the translation by Tagore which, though very free, does not miss the emphasis.

1. *On God*

"Thou art That" is the preaching of the Upaniṣads; that is their message.

Great is their reliance upon this; but how can they, however mighty, describe Him?

Pandit, your thoughts are all untrue; there is here no universe and no creator;
Nor subtle, nor gross, nor air, nor fire, nor sun, nor moon, nor earth, nor water;
Nor the form of light, nor time are there; there is neither word nor body.
There is neither action nor virtue, no mantras and no worship at all.
Rites and ceremonies have no worth at all.
He is one, there is no second.

Wherever, wherever one looks, there, there is He the same; He is found in every vessel.

How can I explain His form or outline? there is no second who has seen Him.
How can I describe the condition of the unconditioned, who has neither village nor resting-place?
He who must be seen without qualities; by what name shall I call Him?

When the fire of avarice is out, and the smoke of desires no longer issueth.
[Then shall man know] that one God is everywhere contained, and that there is no second.

The joiner dwelleth ever separate from the work.[47]

2. *Asceticism*

Some shave men's locks and hang the black cord on their necks,
And pride themselves on the practice of Yoga.
What credit is there in causing your seat to fly?
Crow and kite also circle in the air.

Sitting on the air, studying Yoga, Vedas, rites and astrology, they are demented.
Kabīr says, The hope of the Yogī and the Jaṅgama[a] is withered.

The Yogī says: Yoga is best of all; O brother, it has no rival;
Yogīs with plaited hair, or shaven head, with sealed lips or matted locks—where did these find wisdom?

The Yogī says that Yoga and nothing else is good and sweet;
They who shave their bodies, and the Ekśabdīs,[b] say that they alone have obtained perfection.
Without God thou art lost in error, O blind one!

Thou dependest on a club, earrings, and patched coat,
In error thou wanderest in a Yogī's garb.
Put away thy devotional attitudes and thy suspension of breath:
Abandon deception, and ever worship God, O fool![47]

[a] A kind of ascetic.
[b] Another kind of ascetic.

3. *Yearning and Love for God*

Kabīr says: my heart is dying though it lives.

I played day and night with my comrades, and now I am greatly afraid.

So high is my Lord's palace, my heart trembles to mount its stairs: yet I must not be shy, if I would enjoy His love.

My heart must cleave to my Lover: I must withdraw my veil, and meet him with all my body.

Mine eyes must perform the ceremony of the lamps of love.

Kabīr says: "Listen to me, friend: he understands who loves. If you feel not love's longing for your Beloved One, it is vain to adorn your body, vain to put unguent on your eyelids."

The shadows of evening fall thick and deep, and the darkness of love envelops the body and the mind.

Open the window to the west, and be lost in the sky of love;

Drink the sweet honey that steeps the petals of the lotus of the heart.

Receive the waves in your body: what splendour is in the region of the sea.

I am wandering yet in the alleys of knowledge without purpose, but I have received His news in these alleys of knowledge.

I have a letter from my Beloved; in this letter is an unutterable message, and now my fear of death is done away.

Kabīr says: "O my loving friend! I have got for my gift the Deathless One."

This day is dear to me above all other days, for to-day the Beloved Lord is a guest in my house;

My chamber and my courtyard are beautiful with His presence;

My longings sing His Name, and they are become lost in His great beauty: I wash His feet, and I look upon His Face and I lay before Him as an offering my body, my mind, and all that I have.

What a day of gladness is that day in which my Beloved, who is my treasure, comes to my house. All evils fly from my heart when I see my Lord.

My love has touched Him; my heart is longing for the Name which is Truth.

Thus sings Kabīr, the servant of all servants.[48]

VIII. Dādū

Belonging to the end of the sixteenth century, the Gujerāti poet Dādū is the author of "*bāṇī*" or versified "words" which served as a basic text for the Dādūpanthīs, a sect named after him.

The Living Dead

Have done with pride and arrogance, conceit, envy, self-assertion;
Practise humility, obedience; worship the Creator.

When a man has abandoned false pride, arrogance, and vainglory,
When he has become humble and meek, then does he find true bliss.

Prince and beggar alike must die: not one survives.
Him do thou call living who has died and yet lives.

My enemy "I" is dead: now none can smite me down.
'Tis I who slay myself: thus, being dead, I live.

We have slain our enemy, we have died; but he is not forgotten.
The thorn remains to vex us. Consider and lay this truth to heart.

Then only wilt thou find the Beloved when thou art as the living dead;
Only by losing thyself canst thou find Him who knoweth all.

Then wilt thou find the Beloved, when thou esteemest thyself as nothing;
Recognise therefore by quiet reflection whence the thought of self arises.

Becoming as the living dead, come thou into the way.
First lay down thy head, then mayest thou venture to plant thy foot.

Know that the way of discipleship is exceeding hard;
The living dead walk in it, the Name of Rāma their sign.

So difficult is the way, no living man can tread it;
He only can walk in it, O foolish one, who has died and lives.

Only he who is dead can tread the way that leads to Nirañjana;[a]
He finds the Beloved, and leaps the fearsome gulf.

He that is alive shall die: only by dying inwardly shall he meet the Lord;
Forsaking His fellowship who can endure when trouble comes?

O when will this dominion of self pass away? When will the heart forget every other?
When will it be wholly refined? When will it find its true home?

When I am not, then there is one; when I intrude, then two.
When the curtain of "I" and "you" is drawn aside, then do I become even as I was.[49]

[a] Śiva.

IX. Caitanya

Caitanya (1485–1533) was the founder of a sect in Bengel. He lauds Kṛṣṇa and Rādhā (wife of the god) in the famous *saṃkīrtanas,* hymns sung in chorus. The main part of the literary works of the sect have been composed by disciples of Caitanya; they develop a very elaborate *bhakti* with a more or less erotic tendency which results for some in a Kṛṣṇaite Tântrism.

A Bhakti Shorter Catechism

Question. Which knowledge is the highest of all?
Answer. There is no knowledge but devotion to Kṛṣṇa.

Qu. What is the highest glory in all types of glory?
A. Being reputed to be Kṛṣṇa's devotee.

Qu. What is counted wealth among human possessions?
A. He is immensely wealthy who has love for Rādhā-Kṛṣṇa.

Qu. What is the heaviest of all sorrows?
A. There is no sorrow except separation from Kṛṣṇa.

Qu. Who is considered liberated among those who are liberated?
A. He is the foremost of the liberated who practises devotion to Kṛṣṇa.

Qu. Among songs what song is natural to creatures?
A. It is the song whose heart is the love-sports of Rādhā-Kṛṣṇa.

Qu. What is the highest good of all creatures?
A. There is none except the society of those who are devoted to Kṛṣṇa.

Qu. Whom do creatures incessantly remember?
A. The chief things to be remembered are Kṛṣṇa's name, qualities and sports.

Qu. Among objects of meditation which should creatures meditate on?
A. The supreme meditation is on the lotus-feet of Rādhā-Kṛṣṇa.

Qu. Where should creatures live leaving all behind?
A. It is the glorious land of Brindâban[a] where the *rās-līlâ*[b] is eternal.

Qu. What is the best of things to be heard by creatures?
A. The Rādhā-Kṛṣṇa love sports are a delight to the ear.

Qu. What is chief among the objects of worship?
A. The name of the most adorable couple, Rādhā-Kṛṣṇa.[50]

[a] Place where Kṛṣṇa passed his youth.
[b] Kṛṣṇa's dance.

X. Tulsīdās

The name of Tulsīdās (d. 1623) dominates the religious poetry of modern India. His main work (in Hindī) is the *Rāmacaritmānas* ("Sacred Lake of the Acts of Rāma"), a sort of lyrical epic liberally inspired by the *Rāmāyaṇa* and more particularly by the *Adhyātma-Rāmāyaṇa.* In this work, Rāma is the supreme God who for love of human beings incarnated himself as a fabulous hero. This poem serves as a Bible, it has been said, for a hundred million men, and its popularity has spread beyond the boundaries of the territory of the Hindī language.

1. *The Sermon of God Śiva*

Listen to me, O Pārvatī,[a] and my speech shall dispel error as the sun scatters darkness away.

There is no difference between the Personal and the Impersonal: so they say, the sages, the ascetics, the Vedas, and the *Purāṇas.*[b] He who is Impersonal, without form and unborn becomes Personal for love of his devotees. But how is it that the Impersonal could become Personal? Just as water transforms itself into ice.

Rāma is the Sun, the true Being, Consciousness, Bliss; him the night of Delusion touches not. He is the Fundamental Light, the Adorable: how shall there be a dawn of wisdom for him? Happiness and Misery, Knowledge and Ignorance, Conceit and Pride are the lot of mortal men, but Rāma, as all the world knows, is the Omnipresent Absolute, Supreme Bliss, Lord over all, and everlasting.

He is the renowned Spirit, the Treasure of Light, a manifestation of the Lord of the Universe, Jewel of the Solar race, and my Master. Saying thus, Śiva bowed his head.

The ignorant do not understand their own error and, in their stupidity, they attribute their delusion to the Lord: like fools looking at the sky covered by clouds they say that the sun is covered, or looking at the moon through their fingers pressed on the eyes they imagine that there are two moons. O Umā,[c] such delusion does not affect Rāma as obscurity, smoke and dust do not affect the sky.

Objects of senses, the senses, the deities of the senses, and the individual souls each depend on the next for their conscious existence, but he who illuminates them all, he is the eternal Rāma, prince of Ayodhyā. All that is illuminable is illuminated by Rāma. He is lord of Māyā,[d] and possesses all wisdom and virtue: by his reality does inactive Māyā borrow an air of Reality with the help of Delusion. Because like the brilliance of an oyster shell, like a mirage in the rays of the sun, error is unreal and still none can ever escape it.

Thus the world depends on Hari[e] and though unreal, it can cause suffering: like a man who dreams that his head is cut suffers till he awakes.

He by whose favour such error is corrected, O Pārvatī, is that gracious Rāma. In Him is no beginning, no end, and the Vedas have tried their best to describe him thus: "Without feet he walks, without ears he hears, without hands he performs his various deeds, without palate he perceives all tastes, without speech he is the most eloquent, without body he touches, without eyes he sees, without nose he smells all odour: thus his activity is supernatural in all ways and none can describe his greatness."[51]

(*Rāmacaritmānas*, 1.115 ff.)

[a] Śiva's consort.
[b] Sacred Books of the Hindus.
[c] Pārvatī.
[d] Cosmic illusion.
[e] Viṣṇu.

2. *Praise of Rāma as the Supreme Being*

You are the guardian of the bounds of revelation, O Rāma, you are the Lord of the Universe, and Jānakī[a] is Māyā[b] which creates, preserves and destroys the world at your pleasure, O All Gracious. And Lakṣmaṇa[c] is the Serpent with thousand hoods who supports the earth, sovereign of all things animate and inanimate. You have taken a human body for the good of Gods and you have come to destroy the army of demons.

Your real form transcends speech and intelligence. You are ineffable and infinite, called ever by the Vedas: "Not this! not this!" The world is only a drama and you watch it as a spectator, and Brahmā, Viṣṇu, and Śiva you make to dance like puppets. They themselves know not the mystery of your character: who else can then understand you as you are? He alone knows you to whom you have granted the power to know you, and knowing you he becomes one with you.

It is by your Grace, O Raghunandan, that your devotees understand you, you touch the heart of the faithful like refreshing sandalpaste. Your true form is pure thought and bliss, free from change. They know it who have been privileged thus. But for the good of gods and the just, you have taken the form of illusion and you speak and act as a prince of this earth.

O Rāma, when they see your actions and when they hear about them, fools are perplexed, but the saints rejoice; whatever you say or do is right: like costume, like mimicry.[52]

[a] Rāma's wife.
[b] Cosmic illusion.
[c] Rāma's brother.

XI. Rāmaprasād Sen

This Bengali poet (1718–1775) was the author of odes which were addressed to the Goddess and attest to a profound mystical sentiment.

1. *Death at Hand*

Consider this, my Soul, that thou hast none whom thou mayest call thine own. Vain are thy wanderings on the earth. Two days or three, then ends this earthly life; yet all men boast that they are masters here. Time's master, Death, will come and overthrow such masterships. Thy best-beloved, for whom thou art so terribly concerned, will she go with thee? Nay; rather, lest some ill befall the home, she will sprinkle with cowdung[a] the house where thou hast died.

[a] Cowdung is used in Hindu houses for purification.

2. *Preparation for Death*

Soul, why hast thou become a beggar? Thrice-wretched, knowing nought?

In search of the wealth that passes, thou art wandering from land to land. That which thou desirest, which thou lovest, seest thou not within thine home?

Soul, if thou but quit thyself like mind, thou shalt come to union. When worship comes easy and natural as thy breath, then death's poison will have no power upon thee.

The jewels and the wealth thy teachers have given, bind them fast to thee.

This is the request of poor Rāmaprasād, who hopes to touch the Feet that banish fear.

3. *All Error is Ended*

No more shall I wander and live amid error. I have rested all upon the Feet that banish fear, and with fear I shall not shake again. Weighted no more with the worldly passions that beset me, I shall not sink into the well of poison. Regarding joy and teen alike, I shall no more carry fire in my mind. Drunk with desire of worldly wealth no longer, I shall not wander from door to door. I shall not clutch at the wind of hope, and lay bare my mind to others. Being now no more captive to the snares of sense, I shall not swing myself beneath love's Tree.

4. *The End*

Tārā,[a] do you remember any more?

Mother, as I have lived happy, is there happiness hereafter? Had Śiva's words been true, I should not be beseeching you. After passing through delusion on delusion, I feel my right eyelid throbbing.

Had there been any other place, I should not have besought you. But now, Mother, having given me hope, you have cut my bonds, you have lifted me to the tree's top.

Rāmaprasād says: My mind is firm, and my gift to the priest[b] well made. Mother, my Mother, my all is finished. I have offered my gift.[c]

(Nos. 51, 54, 63, 65)

[a] The goddess.

[b] The gift (in this case, Rāmaprasād's gift of his devotion) when worship is ended.

[c] "I owe a cock to Aesculapius"—Socrates.

XII. Rāmmohun Roy

A Bengali Brahmin, Rāmmohun Roy (1772–1833) was apparently the first Indian to look for a contact with Western culture. Loyally attached to Hindu Scriptures, he studied Christian source books with no less interest, and he attempted to make use of their ethical monotheistic ideal to infuse a new life into traditional Hinduism. He has been quite rightly called the "Father of Modern India."

Hinduism Is Not Inferior to Christianity

If by the "ray of intelligence" for which the Christian says we are indebted to the English, he means the introduction of useful mechanical arts, I am ready to express my assent and also my gratitude; but with respect to science, literature, or religion, I do not acknowledge that we are placed under any obligation. For by a reference to History it may be proved that the world was indebted to our ancestors for the first dawn of knowledge, which sprang up in the East, and thanks to the Goddess of Wisdom, we have still a philosophical and copious language of our own which distinguishes us from other nations who cannot express scientific or abstract ideas without borrowing the language of foreigners. . . .

Before "A Christian" indulged in a tirade about persons being "degraded by *Asiatic* effeminacy," he should have recollected that almost all the ancient prophets and patriarchs venerated by Christians, nay even Jesus Christ himself, a Divine Incarnation and the *founder* of the Christian Faith, were Asiatics. So that if a Christian thinks it degrading to be born or to reside in Asia, he directly reflects upon them. . . .

It is unjust in the Christian to quarrel with Hindoos because (he says) they cannot comprehend the sublime mystery of his religion; since he is equally unable to comprehend the sublime mysteries of ours, and since both these mysteries equally transcend the human understanding, one cannot be preferred to the other.[54]

XIII. Rāmakrishna

Born in a village of Bengal, Rāmakrishna (1836–1886) had a mystical experience which apparently was quite a rare one and which accorded him, without his wishing it, a spiritual status that his more cultured contemporaries could have envied. His devotion is characterized by an unrestricted nonsectarian Hinduism: the cult of the Mother, however, seems to predominate.

The World as Seen by a Mystic

I practised austerities for a long time. I cared very little for the body. My longing for the Divine Mother was so great that I would not eat or sleep. I would lie on the bare ground, placing my head on a lump of earth, and cry out loudly: "Mother, Mother, why dost Thou not come to me?" I did not know how the days and nights passed away. I used to have ecstasy all the time. I saw my disciples as my own people, like children and relations, long before they came to me. I used to cry before my Mother, saying: "O Mother! I am dying for my beloved ones; do Thou bring them to me as quickly as possible."

At that time whatever I desired came to pass. Once I desired to build a small hut in the Panchavati[a] for meditation and to put a fence around it. Immediately after I saw a huge bundle of bamboo sticks, rope, strings, and even a knife, all brought by the tide in front of the Panchavati. A servant of the Temple, seeing these things, ran to me with great delight and told me of them. There was the exact quantity of material necessary for the hut and the fence. When they were built, nothing remained over. Everyone was amazed to see this wonderful sight.

When I reached the state of continuous ecstasy, I gave up all external forms of worship; I could no longer perform them. Then I prayed to my Divine Mother: "Mother, who will now take care of me? I have no power to take care of myself. I like to hear Thy name and feed Thy beloved ones and help the poor. Who will make it possible for me to do these things? Send me someone who will be able to do these for me." As the answer to this prayer came Mathura Bābu,[b] who served me so long and with such intense devotion and faith! Again at another time I said to the Mother: "I shall have no child of my own, but I wish to have as my child a pure Bhakta,[c] who will stay with me all the time. Send me such an one."

In referring to the time of joyous illumination which immediately followed His enlightenment, He exclaimed:

What a state it was! The slightest cause aroused in me the thought of the Divine Ideal. One day I went to the Zoological Garden in Calcutta. I desired especially to see the lion, but when I beheld him, I lost all sense-consciousness and went into samādhi. Those who were with me wished to show me the other animals, but I replied: "I saw everything when I saw the king of beasts. Take me home." The strength of the lion had aroused in me the consciousness of the omnipotence of God and had lifted me above the world of phenomena.

Another day I went to the parade ground to see the ascension of a balloon. Suddenly my eyes fell upon a young English boy leaning against a tree. The very posture of his body brought before me the vision of the form of Kṛṣṇa and I went into *samādhi*.[d]

Again I saw a woman wearing a blue garment under a tree. She was a harlot. As I looked at her, instantly the ideal of Sītā[e] appeared before me! I forgot the existence of the harlot, but saw before me pure and spotless Sītā, approached Rāma, the Incarnation of Divinity, and for a long time I remained motionless. I worshipped all women as representatives of the Divine Mother. I realized the Mother of the universe in every woman's form.

Mathura Bābu, the son-in-law of Râshmoni, invited me to stay in his house for a few days. At that time I felt so strongly that I was the maid-servant of my Divine Mother that I thought of myself as a woman. The ladies of the house had the same feeling; they did not look upon me as a man. As women are free before a young girl, so were they before me. My mind was above the consciousness of sex.

What a Divine state it was! I could not eat here in the

Temple. I would walk from place to place and enter into the house of strangers after their meal hour. I would sit there quietly, without uttering a word. When questioned, I would say: "I wish to eat here." Immediately they would feed me with the best things they had.[55]

[a] Five sacred trees planted together to form a grove for contemplation.

[b] A wealthy disciple.

[c] A devotee.

[d] Mystic contemplation.

[e] The consort of Rāma: she exemplifies the Hindu ideal of womanhood.

XIV. Vivekānanda

Swāmī ("Lord") Vivekānanda (1863–1902) was born and died at Calcutta. He was the most dynamic of all the disciples of Rāmakrishna, and took upon himself something of a missionary vocation. He founded in India the Rāmakrishna Mission, which has been devoted particularly to philanthropic activities. During his travels in Europe and in America he attempted to promote the idea of a kind of universal religion founded on a *Vedānta* which might be adapted to the needs of our times.

Indian Thought to Conquer the World

This is the great ideal before us, and every one must be ready for it—the conquest of the whole world by India—nothing less than that, and we must all get ready for it, strain every nerve for it. Let foreigners come and flood the land with their armies, never mind. Up, India, and conquer the world with your spirituality! Aye, as has been declared on this soil first, love must conquer hatred, hatred cannot conquer itself. Materialism and all its miseries can never be conquered by materialism. Armies when they attempt to conquer armies only multiply and make brutes of humanity. Spirituality must conquer the West. Slowly they are finding out that what they want is spirituality to preserve them as nations. They are waiting for it, they are eager for it. Where is the supply to come from? Where are the men ready to go out to every country in the world with the messages of the great sages of India? Where are the men who are ready to sacrifice everything, so that this message shall reach every corner of the world? Such heroic souls are wanted to help the spread of truth. Such heroic workers are wanted to go abroad and help; to disseminate the great truths of the *Vedānta*. The world wants it; without it the world will be destroyed. The whole of the Western world is on a volcano which may burst tomorrow, go to pieces tomorrow. They have searched every corner of the world and have found no respite. They have drunk deep of the cup of pleasure and found it vanity. Now is the time to work so that India's spiritual ideas may penetrate deep into the West. Therefore, young men of Madras, I specially ask you to remember this. We must go out, we must conquer the world through our spirituality and philosophy. There is no other alternative, we must do it or die. The only condition of national life, of awakened and vigorous national life, is the conquest of the world by Indian thought.[56]

XV. Tagore

Rabīndranāth Tagore (1861–1941), lyrical poet, novelist, dramatist and essayist (he was also a musician and an artist), was an eminent representative of the new Indian humanism. He preached a harmony between the cultures of the orient and the occident, and tried to awaken in men a kind of spiritually beyond all precise belief, one which could be based on an understanding among peoples and the sentiment of human equality. Nevertheless, his Hindu background and sentimentality are undeniable, as can be seen from the poem we reproduce below. This poem is inspired by a motif known from the *Purāṇas:* When the ocean was churned to recover the lost nectar of immortality, Urvaśī, a nymph of entrancing beauty, rose from it. She became the chief dancing girl in Indra's heaven.

Urvasi, or Ideal Beauty

Thou art not Mother, art not Daughter, are not Bride, thou beautiful comely One,
O Dweller in Paradise, Urvasi!
When Evening descends on the pastures, drawing about her tired body her golden cloth,
Thou lightest the lamp within no home.
With hesitant wavering steps, with throbbing breast and downcast look,
Thou dost not go smiling to any Beloved's bed,
In the hushed midnight.
Thou art unveiled like the rising Dawn,
Unshrinking One!

Like some stemless flower, blooming in thyself,
When didst thou blossom, Urvasi?
That primal Spring, thou didst arise from the churning of Ocean,
Nectar in thy right hand, venom in thy left.[a]
The swelling mighty Sea, like a serpent tamed with spells,
Drooping his thousand towering hoods,
Fell at thy feet!

White as the kunda-blossom, a naked beauty, adored by the King of the Gods,
Thou flawless One!

Wast thou never bud, never maiden of tender years,
O eternally youthful Urvasi?
Sitting alone, under whose dark roof
Didst thou know childhood's play, toying with gems and pearls?
At whose side, in what chamber lit with the flashing of gems,
Lulled by the sea-waves' chant, didst thou sleep on coral bed,
A smile on thy pure face?
That moment when thou awakedst into the Universe, thou wast framed of youth,
In full-blown beauty!

From age to age thou hast been the world's beloved,
O unsurpassed in loveliness, Urvasi!
Breaking their meditation,[b] sages lay at thy feet the fruits of their penance;
Smitten with thy glance, the three worlds grow restless with youth;
The blinded winds blow thine intoxicating fragrance around;
Like the black bee, honey-drunken, the infatuated poet wanders, with greedy heart,
Lifting chants of wild jubilation!
While thou goest, with jingling anklets and waving skirts,
Restless as lightning!

In the assembly of the Gods, when thou dancest in ecstasy of joy,
O swaying wave, Urvasi!
The companies of billows in mid-ocean swell and dance, beat on beat;
In the crests of the corn the skirts of Earth tremble;
From thy necklace stars fall off in the sky;
Suddenly in the breast of man the heart forgets itself,
The blood dances!

Suddenly in the horizon thy zone bursts—
Ah, wild in abandon!

On the Sunrise Mount in Heaven thou art the embodied Dawn,
O world-enchanting Urvasi!
Thy slender form is washed with the streaming tears of the Universe;
The ruddy hue of thy feet is painted with the heart's blood of the three worlds;
Thy tresses escaped from the braid, thou hast placed thy light feet,
Thy lotus-feet, on the Lotus of the blossomed
Desires of the Universe!
Endless are thy masks in the mind's heaven,
O Comrade of dreams!

Hear what crying and weeping everywhere rise for thee,
O cruel, deaf Urvasi!
Say, will that Ancient Prime ever revisit this earth?—
From the shoreless unfathomed deep wilt thou rise again, with wet locks?—
First in the First Dawn that Form will show!
In the startled gaze of the Universe all thy limbs will be weeping,
The waters flowing from them!
Suddenly the vast Sea, in songs never heard before,
Will thunder with its waves!

She will not return, she will not return!—that Moon of Glory has set!
She has made her home on the Mount of Setting, has Urvasi!
Therefore on Earth today with the joyous breath of Spring
Mingles the long-drawn sigh of some eternal separation.
On the night of full moon, when the world brims with laughter,
Memory, from somewhere far away, pipes a flute that brings unrest,

The tears gush out!
Yet in that weeping of the spirit Hope wakes and lives,
Ah, Unfettered One![57]

[a] The nectar and poison both emerged from the churning of the ocean.

[b] Indian legends tell of sages tempted by envious gods to break their penance, before it had made them too powerful.

XVI. Gāndhī

During his long and hard campaign for the independence of India, Mohandās Karamchand Gāndhī (1869–1948) emphasized, above all, the principle of nonviolence. He combined in himself the role of ardent nationalist and the faith of a preacher of a revived Hinduism which would insist on the themes of perfection and purity. He was, in a word, a politician who wagered on becoming a saint.

1. *Through Ahiṃsā*[a] *to God*

My uniform experience has convinced me that there is no other God than Truth. And if every page of these chapters does not proclaim to the reader that the only means for the realization of Truth is non-violence, I shall deem all my labor in writing to have been in vain. And, even though my efforts in this behalf may prove fruitless, let the readers know that the vehicle, not the great principle, is at fault. After all, however sincere my strivings after *Ahiṃsā* may have been, they have still been imperfect and inadequate. The little fleeting glimpses, therefore, that I have been able to have of Truth can hardly convey an idea of the indescribable luster of Truth, a million times more intense than that of the sun we daily see with our eyes. In fact what I have caught is only the faintest glimmer of that mighty effulgence. But this much I can say with assurance, as a result of all my experiments, that a perfect vision of Truth can only follow a complete realization of *Ahiṃsā*.

To see the universal and all-pervading Spirit of Truth face to face one must be able to love the meanest of creation as oneself. And a man who aspires after that cannot afford to keep out of any field of life. That is why my devotion to Truth has drawn me into the field of politics; and I can say without the slightest hesitation, and yet in all humility, that those who say that religion has nothing to do with politics do not know what religion means.

Identification with everything that lives is impossible without self-purification; without self-purification the observance of the law of *Ahiṃsā* must remain an empty dream; God can never be realized by one who is not pure of heart. Self-purification therefore must mean purification in all the walks of life. And purification being highly infectious, purification of oneself necessarily leads to the purification of one's surroundings.

But the path of self-purification is hard and steep. To attain to perfect purity one has to become absolutely passion-free in thought, speech, and action; to rise above the opposing currents of love and hatred, attachment and repulsion. I know that I have not in me as yet that triple purity, in spite of constant ceaseless striving for it. That is why the world's praise fails to move me, indeed it very often stings me. To conquer the subtle passions seems to me to be harder far than the physical conquest of the world by the force of arms. Ever since my return to India I have had experiences of the dormant passions lying hidden within me. The knowledge of them has made me feel humiliated though not defeated. The experiences and experiments have sustained me and given me a great joy. But I know that I have still before me a difficult path to traverse. I must reduce myself to zero. So long as a man does not of his own free will put himself last among his fellow creatures, there is no salvation for him. *Ahiṃsā* is the farthest limit of humility.

In bidding farewell to the reader, for the time being at any rate, I ask him to join with me in prayer to the God of Truth that He may grant me the boon of *Ahiṃsā* in mind, word, and deed.[58]

[a] Nonviolence.

2. *God's Name*

It is a sun that has brightened my darkest hours. Rāma's name is no copybook maxim. It is something that has to be realized through experience. One who has had personal experience alone can prescribe it, not any other. The recitation of Rāma's name for spiritual ailments is as old as the hills. But the greater includes the less. And my claim is that the recitation of Rāma's name is a sovereign remedy for our physical ailments also. We want healers of souls rather than of bodies. The multiplicity of hospitals and of medical men is no sign of civilization. The less we and others pamper our body, the better for us and the world. Rāma's name is for the pure in heart and for those who want to attain purity and remain pure. It can never be a means of self-indulgence. Rāma's name, to be efficacious, must absorb your entire being during its recitation and express itself in your whole life. My Rāma, the Rāma of our prayers, is not the historical Rāma, the son of Daśaratha, the king of Ayodhyā. He is the eternal, the unborn, the one without a second. Rāma's name has the terrible power of converting one's sex-desire into a divine longing for the Lord. Rāma's name if recited from the heart charms away every evil thought.

Hindudharma is like a boundless ocean, teeming with priceless gems. The deeper you dive, the more treasures you find; it is the way trodden by some of the greatest sages of India who were men of God, not superstitious men or charlatans: to take Rāma's name from the heart means deriving help from an incomparable power. The atom-bomb is as nothing compared with it. This power is capable of removing all pain; to say this is easy. To attain the Reality is very difficult. Nevertheless it is the biggest thing man can possess.

Reason follows the heart, it does not guide it. A pure heart is thus the most essential requisite for mental and physical health. Tolstoy said that if man dismissed God from his heart even for a single moment, Satan occupied the vacancy. Rāma's name would expel Satan. By ourselves we are insignificant worms. We become great when we reflect His greatness. Men make a fetish of their physical being while neglecting the immortal Spirit. Anyone who bears Him in his or her heart has accession of a marvellous force or energy as objective in its results as, say electricity, but much subtler. Rāma's name is like a mathematical formula which summed up in brief the result of endless research. What an amount of labour and patience have been lavished by men to acquire the non-existent philosopher's stone. Surely, God's name is of infinitely richer value and always existent.[59]

XVII. Aurobindo

After a short period spent in the political struggle for independence, Aurobindo Ghose (1872–1950) devoted himself to spiritual practices in the Āśram at Pondichéry. He published a great number of works of a semireligious, semiphilosophical character, notable among which were a reinterpretation of the Veda and commentaries on the *Upaniṣads* and other texts of a free Vedântic inspiration.

1. *The Resurrection of Hinduism*

What is the Hindu religion? What is this religion which we call Sanatan, eternal? It is the Hindu religion only because the Hindu nation has kept it, because in this Peninsula it grew up in the seclusion of the sea and the Himalayas, because in this sacred and ancient land it was given as a charge to the Aryan race to preserve through the ages. But it is not circumscribed by the confines of a single country, it does not belong peculiarly and forever to a bounded part of the world. That which we call the Hindu religion is really the eternal religion, because it is the universal religion which embraces all others. If a religion is not universal, it cannot be eternal. A narrow religion, a sectarian religion, an exclusive religion can live only for a limited time and a limited purpose. This is the one religion that can triumph over materialism by including and anticipating the discoveries of science and the speculations of philosophy. It is the one religion which impresses on mankind the closeness of God to us and embraces in its compass all the possible means by which man can approach God. It is the one religion which insists every moment on the truth which all religions acknowledge that He is in all men and all things and that in Him we move and have our being. It is the one religion which enables us not only to understand and believe this truth but to realize it with every part of our being. It is the one religion which shows the world what the world is, that is the Sport of God. It is the one religion which shows us how we can best play our part in that Sport, its subtlest laws and its noblest rules. It is the one religion which does not separate life in any smallest detail from religion, which knows what immortality is and has utterly removed from us the reality of death.

This is the word that has been put into my mouth to speak to you today. What I intended to speak has been put away from me, and beyond what is given to me I have nothing to say. It is only the word that is put into me that I can speak to you. That word is now finished. I spoke once before with this force in me and I said then that this movement is not a political movement and that nationalism is not politics but a religion, a creed, a faith. I say it again today, but I put it in another way. I say no longer that nationalism is a creed, a religion, a faith; I say that it is the Sanatan Dharma[a] which for us is nationalism. This Hindu nation was born with the Sanatan Dharma, with it it moves and with it it grows. When the Sanatan Dharma declines, then the nation declines, and if the Sanatan Dharma were capable of perishing, with the Sanatan Dharma it would perish. The Sanatan Dharma that is nationalism. This is the message that I have to speak to you.[60]

[a] Literally, "the Eternal Law."

2. *The Spiritual Life*

It is almost universally supposed that spiritual life must necessarily be a life of ascetic spareness, a pushing away of all that is not absolutely needed for the bare maintenance of the body; and this is valid for a spiritual life which is in its nature and intention a life of withdrawal from life. Even apart from that ideal, it might be thought that the spiritual turn must always make for an extreme simplicity, because all else would be a life of vital desire and physical self-indulgence. But from a wider standpoint this is a mental standard based on the law of the ignorance of which desire is the motive; to overcome the ignorance, to delete the ego, a total rejection not only of desire but of all the things that can satisfy may intervene as a valid principle. But this standard or any mental standard cannot be absolute nor can it be binding as a law on the consciousness that has risen above desire; a complete purity and self-mastery would be in the very grain of its nature and that would remain the same in poverty or in riches: for if it could be shaken or sullied by either, it would not be real or would not be complete. The one rule of the gnostic life would be the self-expression of the Spirit, the will of the Divine Being; that will, that self-expression could manifest through extreme simplicity or through extreme complexity and opulence or in their natural balance,—for beauty and plenitude, a hidden sweetness and laughter in things, a sunshine and gladness of life are also powers and expressions of the Spirit. In all directions the spirit within determining the law of the nature would determine the frame of the life and its detail and circumstance. In all there would be the same plastic principle; a rigid standardisation, however necessary for the mind's arrangement of things, could not be the law of the spiritual life. A great diversity and liberty of self-expression based on an underlying unity might well become manifest; but everywhere there would be harmony and truth of order.[61]

XVIII. Radhakrishnan

Born in 1888, Sir Sarvapalli Radhakrishnan, now Vice-President of the Indian Republic, is the most remarkable of the philosophers and religious thinkers of modern India. He has tried to establish, in his own way, a connection between Indian thought (based on *Vedānta* and Buddhism) and Western thought, without, however, sacrificing anything of the main Hindu theories.

Salvation

It is the aim of religion to lift us from our momentary meaningless provincialism to the significance and status of the eternal, to transform the chaos and confusion of life to that pure and immortal essence which is its ideal possibility. If the human mind so changes itself as to be perpetually in the glory of the divine light, if the human emotions transform themselves into the measure and movement of the divine bliss, if human action partakes of the creativity of the divine life, if the human life shares the purity of the divine essence, if only we can support this higher life, the long labour of the cosmic process will receive its crowning justification and the evolution of centuries unfold its profound significance. The divinising of the life of man in the individual and the race is the dream of the great religions. It is the *mokṣa*[a] of the Hindus, the *nirvāṇa* of the Buddhists, the kingdom of heaven of the Christians. It is for Plato the life of the untroubled perception of the pure idea. It is the realisation of one's native form, the restoration of one's integrity of being. Heaven is not a place where God lives but an order of being, a world of spirit where the ideas of wisdom, love and beauty exist eternally, a kingdom into which we may enter at once in spirit, which we can realize fully in ourselves and in society though only by long and patient effort. The expectation of the second advent is the expression of the soul's conviction of the reality of the spiritual. The world process reaches its consummation when every man knows himself to be the immortal spirit, the son of God and is it. Till this goal is reached, each saved individual is the centre of the universal consciousness. He continues to act without the sense of the ego. To be saved is not to be moved from the world. Salvation is not escape from life. The individual works in the cosmic process no longer as an obscure and limited ego, but as a centre of the divine or universal consciousness embracing and transforming into harmony all individual manifestations. It is to live in the world with one's inward being profoundly modified. The soul takes possession of itself and cannot be shaken from its tranquillity by the attractions and attacks of the world. If the saved individual escape literally from the cosmic process, the world would be forever unredeemed. It would be condemned to remain for all time the scene of unending strife and darkness. The Hindus assert different degrees of liberation, but the complete and final release of all is the ultimate one. The *Bhāgavata Purāṇa*[b] records the following prayer: "I desire not the supreme state with all its eight perfections nor the release from rebirth; may I assume the sorrow of all creatures who suffer and enter into them so that they may be free from grief." The self-fulfilment which they aspire to is inconsistent with the failure to achieve similar results in others. This respect for the individual as individual is not the discovery of modern democracy, so far as the religious sphere is concerned. When the cosmic process results in the revelation of all the sons of God, when all the Lord's people become prophets, when this universal incarnation takes place, the great cosmic rebirth of which nature strives to be delivered will be consummated.[62]

[a] Liberation, or release from the necessity of being reborn.
[b] A celebrated religious book of medieval India.

Translation References, Suggested Readings and Index

Translation References

1. Nicol Macnicol, ed., *Hindu Scriptures* (London: J. M. Dent, 1938), pp. 12, 14–15, 18–19, 20, 28–29, 30–32, 36–37.
2. M. Bloomfield, *Hymns of the Atharva-Veda* (Oxford: Clarendon Press, 1897), pp. 1–2, 22, 62, 88–89, 102, 110, 149, 199–205.
3. J. Eggeling *The Śatapatha-Brāhmaṇa* (Oxford: Clarendon Press, 1900), I, 216–218; IV, 400; V, 12–14.
4. R. E. Hume, *The Thirteen Principal Upanishads* (London: Oxford University Press, 1931), pp. 81–82, 98–102, 136–138, 209–210, 226–228, 318–320, 335–339, 357–358, 362–363.
5. S. Radhakrishnan, *The Principal Upaniṣads* (London: George Allen & Unwin, 1953), pp. 597–607.
6. H. Oldenberg, *The Grhya-Sūtras* (Oxford: Clarendon Press, 1886), I, 164–171.
7. G. Bühler, *The Sacred Books of the East* (2d. ed.; Oxford: Clarendon Press, 1882, 1897), II, 2–5, 234–238; XIV, 1–3, 279–283.
8. G. Bühler, *The Laws of Manu* (Oxford: Clarendon Press, 1886), pp. 2–28, 128–131, 166, 195–198, 204–206, 219–220, 483–485.
9. J. Jolly, *The Institutes of Vishnu* (Oxford: Clarendon Press, 1900), pp. 81–83.
10. J. Jolly, *The Minor Law-Books* (Oxford: Clarendon Press, 1889), I, 93–94.
11. S. Radhakrishnan, *The Bhagavad-gītā* (London: George Allen & Unwin, 1948), pp. 98–111, 122–129.
12. F. Edgerton, tr., *The Bhagavad-Gītā* (Cambridge, Mass.: Harvard University Press, 1944), pp. 65–67, 108–119.
13. Sir Edwin Arnold, *The Song Celestial*, quoted from F. Edgerton, *ibid.*, II, 159.
14. J. Muir, *Original Sanskrit Texts* (2d. ed.; London: Trübner & Co., 1872), I, 139–142.
15. M. Monier-Williams, *Indian Wisdom* (3rd ed.; London: Allen, 1876), pp. 412–416.
16. Pratap Chandra Roy, *The Mahabharata* (Calcutta: Dotta Bose, n.d.), II, 66–67.
17. *Ibid.*, pp. 68–69.
18. Summarized from J. Ph. Vogel, *Indian Serpent-Lore* (London: A. Probsthain, 1926), pp. 69–71.
19. Abridged translation from M. Winternitz, *A History of Indian Literature* (Calcutta: University, 1927), I, 408.
20. M. Monier-Williams, *op. cit.*, pp. 350–353.

21. J. Muir, *Metrical Translations from Sanskrit Writers* (London: Trübner & Co., 1871), pp. 41–42.
22. F. E. Pargiter, *The Mārkaṇḍaya-Purāṇa* (Calcutta: Asiatic Society, 1904), pp. 512, 516–517.
23. *Ibid.*, pp. 75, 88–91.
24. H. H. Wilson, *The Vishnu Purāṇa* (London: Trübner, 1864), II, 94.
25. *Ibid.*, I, 143–147, 150.
26. *Ibid.*, III, 76–78.
27. A. Daniélou, *Le polythéisme hindou* (Paris: Corrêa, 1960), p. 422.
28. A. Avalon, *The Great Liberation* (Madras: Ganesh & Co., 1927), pp. 324–338.
29. W. Norman Brown, *The Saundaryalahari* (Cambridge, Mass.: Harvard University Press, 1958), pp. 50, 52, 56.
30. A. L. Basham, *The Wonder That Was India* (London: Sidgwick and Jackson, 1954), pp. 421–422.
31. J. Brough, *Selections from Classical Sanskrit Literature* (London: Luzac & Co., 1952), pp. 101–103.
32. A. L. Basham, *op. cit.*, p. 425.
33. J. Muir, *op. cit.*, pp. 37, 44–45.
34. M. Monier-Williams, *op. cit.*, p. 512.
35 H. H. Wilson, *Select Specimens of the Theatre of the Hindus* (2d. ed.; London: Trübner & Co., 1835), pp. 53–55.
36. J. A. B. Van Buitenen, *Ramanuja on the Bhgavad-gītā* (The Hague: H. L. Smits, 1953), pp. 115–118.
37. A. L. Basham, *op. cit.*, p. 428.
38. J. Brough, *op. cit.*, pp. 81–82.
39. E. B. Cowell and A. E. Gough, *The Sarva-darśana-saṃgraha* (London: Kegan Paul, Trench, Trübner & Co., 1904), pp. 10–11.
40. Editor's translation.
41. F. Kingsbury and G. E. Phillips, *Hymns of the Tamil Śaivite Saints* (Calcutta: Association Press, 1921), pp. 47–51, 65.
42. *Ibid.*, pp. 121 ff., *passim*.
43. J. S. M. Hooper, *Hymns of the Alvars* (Calcutta: Association Press, 1929), pp. 61–64.
44. Gordon Matthews, *Śiva* (New York: Oxford University Press, 1948), p. 81.
45. R. C. Temple, *The Word of Lalla the Prophetess* (Cambridge, Mass.: Cambridge University Press, 1924), pp. 167–173.
46. Freely rendered by Nicol Macnicol, *Psalms of Marâṭha Saints* (Calcutta: Association Press, n.d.), pp. 47, 58, 64, 65, 67, 76.
47. F. E. Keay, *Kabīr and His Followers* (Calcutta: Association Press, 1931), pp. 72, 75.

48. R. Tagore, *One Hundred Poems of Kabīr*, quoted from *North Indian Saints* (Madras: G. A. Natesan, n.d.), pp. 27–28.
49. W. G. Orr, *A Sixteenth-Century Indian Mystic* (London: Lutterworth Press, 1947), pp. 105–106.
50. Melville T. Kennedy, *The Chaitanya Movement* (Calcutta: Association Press, 1925), p. 115.
51. Editor's translation.
52. Editor's translation.
53. E. J. Thompson and A. Marshman Spencer, *Bengali Religious Lyrics* (Calcutta: Association Press, 1923), pp. 62 ff., *passim.*
54. *The English Works of Raja Rammohun Roy* (Allahabad: The Panini Office, 1906), pp. 906, 908.
55. *The Gospel of Ramakrishna* (New York: The Vedanta Society, 1907), pp. 207, 209.
56. Vivekananda, *The Complete Works* (Almora: Advaita Āshrama, 1924–32), III, 276.
57. Quoted from E. Thompson, *R. Tagore* (London: University Press, 1926).
58. Gandhi, *An Autobiography*, trans. Mahadev Desai (Ahmedabad: Navajivan, 1927), pp. 615–617.
59. Translation from *Râmanâma, the Infallible Remedy* (Karachi, 1947), *passim.* Quoted through H. Jacobs, *Western Psychotherapy and Hindu-Sadhana* (London: G. Allen & Unwin, 1961), pp. 112–114.
60. Aurobindo Ghose, *Speeches* (Calcutta: Arya Publishing House, 1948), p. 78.
61. Aurobindo Ghose, *The Life Divine* (3d. ed.; Calcutta: Arya Publishing House, 1947), pp. 944–945.
62. Sarvapalli Radhakrishnan, *An Idealist View of Life* (London: George Allen & Unwin, 1929), Chap. III.

Suggested Readings

A. A number of general books on Indian Civilization deal in more or less detail with facts on Hindu religion. The following are noteworthy:

The History and Culture of the Indian People (Bombay, 1951 et seq.). Six volumes of this work have already appeared.

L. Renou, *L'Inde classique* (Paris, 1949), Vol. I, pp. 270 ff. A manual of Indian studies.

L. D. Barnett, *Antiquities of India* (London, 1913).

A. L. Basham, *The Wonder that was India* (London, 1954).

B. Among the works devoted to Hinduism (and sometimes simultaneously to Buddhism), the following of recent data are noteworthy:

Various authors, *The Cultural Heritage of India* (Calcutta, 1956), Vol. IV: The Religions.

Satishchandra Chatterjee, *The Fundamentals of Hinduism* (Calcutta, 1950).

H. von Glasenapp, *Die Religionen Indiens* (Stuttgart, 1943).

K. W. Morgan, *The Religion of the Hindus* (New York, 1953).

C. Eliot, *Hinduism and Buddhism* (London, 1954), 3 vols.

Comparatively older, but valuable from the point of view of chronology:

J. N. Farquhar, *An Outline of the Religious Literature of India* (Oxford, 1920).

J. Gonda, *Die Religionen Indiens* (Stuttgart, 1960).

The following, in spite of their dates, may still be consulted:

A. Barth, *Les religions de l'Inde* (Paris, 1879, 1914); English translation, 1921.

M. Monier-Williams, *Brahmanism and Hinduism* (London, 1887, 1891). A recast of a work first published in 1883 under a different title.

R. G. Bhandarkar, *Vaishnavism, Śaivism*, etc. (Strassburg, 1913).

E. W. Hopkins, *Religions of India* (London, 1902).

W. Crooke, "Hinduism," *Encyclopedia of Religion and Ethics.*

H. H. Wilson, *Essays and Lectures on the Religion of the Hindus* (London, 1861–62), 2 vols.

C. Different from the usual approach, but useful and suggestive are:

Max Weber, *Hinduismus und Buddhismus* (Tübingen, 1921); English translation, 1958.

S. Radhakrishnam, *The Hindu View of Life* (London, 1939).

D. S. Varma, *What is Hinduism?* (Benares, 1940).

H. Zimmer, *Mythen und Symbole in indischer Kunst und Kultur* (Zurich, 1942). English translation published.

H. Zimmer, *Maya, der indische Mythus* (Zurich, 1942).

A. Daniélou, *Le polythéisme hindou* (Paris, 1960). English translation scheduled for publication.

D. Among monographs published in recent years:

J. Gonda, *Aspects of Early Vishnuism* (Utrecht, 1954).

J. J. Meyer, *Trilogie altindischer Mächte und Feste der Vegetation* (Zurich-Leipzig, 1937).

J. E. Carpenter, *Theism in Mediaeval India* (London, 1926).

S. B. DasGupta, *Obscure Religious Cults* (Calcutta, 1946).

W. Ruben, *Krishna. Konkordanz und Kommentar der Motive seines Heldenlebens* (Istanbul, 1944).

S. K. De, *Early History of the Vaishnava Faith and Movement in Bengal* (Calcutta, 1942).

J. N. Banerjea, *The Development of Hindu Iconography* (Calcutta, 1956).

D. S. Sarma, *Studies in the Renaissance of Hinduism* (Benares, 1944).

L. Dumont, *Le renoncement dans les religions de l'Inde* (Paris, 1959), in *Archives de Sociologie des Religions*, no. 7.

A. Avalon, various works on Tântrism (London, since 1914).

E. Miscellaneous works:

J. Dowson, *A Classical Dictionary of Hindu Mythology and Religion* (London, 1928).

Rabindranath Tagore, *Sādhanā* (Calcutta, 1913).

A. K. Coomaraswamy, *Dance of Śiva* (London, 1918).

F. Selections of translated texts:

J. Muir, *Original Sanskrit Texts* (London, 1858 et seq.), 5 vols.

Various editors, *Sources of Indian Tradition* (New York, 1958).

Sanātana Dharma: An Advanced Text-Book of Hindu Religion and Ethics (Benares, 1904).

The Sacred Books of the East (Oxford, 1879 et seq.).

The Sacred Books of the Hindus (Allahabad, n.d.).

Index